LIVING IN ETERNITY NOW

The 7th Plane of
HEAVEN
and
The Plateau Between
the 7th & 8th Planes

JEANNE REJAUNIER

ISBN-10: 1530785022
ISBN-13: 978-1530785025

DEDICATION

The always smiling, cheerful, sensitive and caring Dr. Fred Adler was throughout many years a vital part of our Friday night Planes of Heaven classes in Pasadena. For all his worldly accomplishments, including being President of the Aerospace Division of Hughes Aircraft where he was in charge of 250,000 employees, Fred was down to earth, humble and unassuming. He was beloved of all his peers, and everybody wanted to be assigned to work for him. Fred Adler raised people up. That's the kind of man he was. His widow, opera singer and voice coach Alise Richal Adler, recalls Fred:

"My beloved husband has left us. This earth angel is now with the heavenly angels. Fred was the kindest, most loving man in the entire world. He stood for all that is good and worthwhile. He was spiritual and wise, with deep wisdom based on love. He was quietly a great human being, as those who knew him will attest. All this, in addition to his outstanding accomplishments. He loved music, art and poetry, but most of all he loved people. It isn't often that someone is born who will touch the world as Fred did. He has commendations from the President of NATO, a scarf from the Dalai Lama, commendations from The City of Hope, to name just a few. He was born March 29, 1925 and left us January 22, 2016. My life began when we met, and he will live in my heart for as long as I am still here. I am so proud to bear his name."

.

CONTENTS

ACKNOWLEDGMENTS

Heartfelt thanks to all the beautiful souls who have passed on since we were together those unforgettable Friday evenings in Pasadena and nights on the other side. Special thanks to the Essene Fellowship of Peace, Simi Valley, CA; to Vadim Newquist for his cover design, and to Sylvia Howe, Pasadena, who painted the portrait of my poodle Gordy and me in front of the Temple of Wisdom.

INTRODUCTION

This is the fifth book in the Planes of Heaven series. If you are a reader new to the study of the Planes, to give you a flavor of what you might expect when you read this current book, here are a few random comments from readers of the four previous volumes:

"A totally new and exciting slant on spirituality..." "A privileged tour beyond the boundaries of any reality we have previously known..." "Groundbreaking ... unlike anything I've ever read before ..." "Examines realms for spiritual enlightenment which earth dwellers may visit nightly in sleep..." "This book is a departure from other books that speak of the Afterlife, because it centers on both life beyond the veil as well as life in the here and now, and shows exactly how the two are interrelated and how readers may connect with life after death in the physical world we live in..." "A highly personal story of a fascinating California spiritual group led by a master teacher."

As the preceding quotes suggest, books in the Planes series explore areas that break new spiritual ground. This fifth book in the series, *Living in Eternity Now*, follows the pattern of its predecessors, building upon them as we enter the 7th Plane of Heaven and the Plateau between the 7th and 8th Planes in preparation for the 8th Plane and the Eightfold Path.

Today more than ever, spiritual seekers are clamoring to know what occurs when we finish this life on Planet Earth. What happens to us? Where do we go? Will we be happy there? Will we rejoin family members who have already crossed to the other side of life? Can we communicate with our departed loved ones right now, and if so, how? What should we do to prepare for our own eventual transition from Earth to that other world?

Every book in the Planes of Heaven series focuses on these and other significant issues, probing from the perspective of numerous seekers of truth of similar mind who, over a period of decades, met Friday evenings in Pasadena, California under the guidance of our inspiring master teacher, Mary Dies Weddell, one of the translators of the Dead Sea Scrolls, whose extensive knowledge of ancient languages, esoteric truth and teachings influenced thousands in America and abroad.

Where did we human beings come from? Where are we going? Why are we here? What is our purpose in life and how may we best fulfill it? If you have ever pondered these and similar enigmas, you are not alone. People throughout the world are sincerely seeking answers, and in particular, they long to know what awaits at the end of our physical lives.

Over past years, the market has been flooded with books on heaven and the afterlife that aptly describe the perfection and harmonious bliss of the world beyond. How do the authors of these books know whereof they write? The majority of titles on heaven and the afterlife are based on their authors' near death experiences (NDE); mediums channeling guides/and or discarnates from the Other Side; messages from the spirit world via automatic writing or clairaudience; past life regressions typically conveyed by subjects under hypnosis or by those who on the operating table have felt the effects of anesthesia which has triggered dormant brainwaves; material channeled by a psychic or clairvoyant person; telepathy; brief, often cryptic Biblical passages subject to interpretation; and/or various combinations thereof.

Most books in the category center around dramatic experiences that were the springboard for the authors' increased knowledge of and faith in life after death, whereas the Planes of Heaven books comprise a fresh, original genre, our group having ventured into unique areas unexplored by other published works on heaven and the afterlife.

The science of nighttime soul travel was central to Mary Weddell's teaching. Having mastered laws governing the ascent and descent

4

of the soul between Heaven and Earth, each night over many years, Mary summoned our spiritual bodies in sleep for training in heaven's temples and halls of learning, and helped us recall our experiences.

Night travel to the heavenly realms is a part of the inner knowledge of all faiths and has been practiced throughout the ages: Indians, Tibetans, Persians, Egyptians, Greeks, Hebrews, Essenes, early Christians, later esoteric Christians and others have avowed the reality of communication between the visible and invisible worlds. The science of nighttime soul travel is mentioned several times in the Bible and by other religions as far back as 10,000 B.C.

Mary Dies Weddell (1886-1980), musician (piano, organ, voice), poet, seer, and philosopher, author of four published books, specialist in Egyptology, hieroglyphics, Sanskrit, Hebrew, Aramaic, and Greek, was a remarkable woman whose teachings I have followed for half a century on both sides of life. The underlying theme of all Mary's work is self knowledge leading to self mastery. Through two peerless original courses, "Creative Color Analysis" and "The Planes of Heaven," Mary enabled us, her students, to see more deeply into ourselves and to understand more fully the awe inspiring structure and purpose of creation here and hereafter. As I wrote of Mary in the first book of the Planes series, *Planes of the Heavenworld*:

"I shall never forget my first glimpse of Mary. Diminutive in stature, large in being, she was radiant, her all-embracing smile spreading a wide arc of wisdom and love. Upon her unexpected entrance, the power that surrounded the group struck a heightened responsive chord, and the energy immediately increased... I felt from the moment I saw Mary that she had the power to show me the unseen things of another world."

From a very early age Mary Weddell was a natural clairvoyant and outstanding medium, gifts she wisely downplayed so that her students might develop their own powers. Mary definitely did not want us to take her word for it, to be parrots who "believed" because she said it was so. Repeatedly, she told us to prove everything for ourselves.

And so, our group of fifty to sixty spiritually interconnecting minds focused on an interplayed joint picture of the myriad areas and levels of heaven and on "climbing" to the next rung in our ongoing search. Thus does this present book continue themes begun in the first four volumes. Now, while we're living here, is the time to become acquainted with that invisible land all of us will some day inhabit, to strengthen ties with the life beyond to which we are all eternally linked, to know its reality, its perfection, its all inclusiveness where all is order, where healing abounds and where love dwells.

Review was always welcome in our Friday night classes. Our subject matter was so vast and all consuming that it could hardly be swallowed in one gulp. From time to time, we would renew the basics, which would always serve to more firmly implant them in our consciousness.

"Color, the Planes, night work, the Teachers, the Sleep World, tests, 'Grand Central Station,' keynotes and keynote colors, the Channel, development, the Hierarchy, missions, color prayer ..." what do they all mean? These and more you will come across as you read this book. If this is your first taste of the Planes teaching, we hope some of the review presented, especially in Part III, will help orient you. But to briefly synopsize:

WHAT ARE THE PLANES OF HEAVEN? The Planes of Heaven are expressions of the soul's growth and progression. We live in two worlds simultaneously, the visible and the invisible. Together, these two separate yet irreparably linked domains comprise the essence of "living in eternity now" and "living in immortality now." The Planes represent the different states and conditions through which an individual soul passes along the way of spiritual ongoing. One comes from the Planes, one lives on after death on the Planes, and one may visit the Planes in sleep.

TEACHERS Spiritual guides, often called teachers or heavenly teachers, help our advancement. A group of teachers administered to the class Friday night; other teachers helped on the other side in our night work, especially assisting in our training and tests.

HIERARCHY Every plane of heaven is supervised by a hierarchy, a group of advanced souls dedicated to helping our spiritual progress.

"GRAND CENTRAL STATION" Mary's term for the place we first land in the Heaven world at night before commencing our temple experiences.

SLEEP WORLD A place those not in spiritual work go in their sleep.

COLOR The Color path is a mystical journey toward soul development. From an advanced state of consciousness, Mary brought through from the Other Side more than one hundred fully tested color rays and their definitions, which form the basis of her unique "Creative Color Analysis" course, which complements work on the Planes.

"THE CHANNEL" or "The Channel of our Being" - The highest spiritual colors, our birthright, are contained in the Channel, also called "the Keys to the Kingdom." This inner portion of a human being is the path of light leading one's consciousness to higher realms of understanding.

MAPS Included in the Planes of Heaven books #2 through #4 are Mary's unique maps/charts of heavenly realms that cite more than one hundred locations in Heaven. This current volume includes two new maps: the 7th Plane and the Plateau between the 7th and 8th Planes. To form a more accurate picture of the Planes, think of these charts as illustrating states of consciousness beyond materiality, as dimensions of being where our spiritual bodies will dwell in the hereafter, which we can also visit every night while living on Earth.

####

*****

For readers unfamiliar with the four previous books in the Planes series, their titles are: *Planes of the Heavenworld; Everything You Always Wanted to Know About Heaven But Didn't Know Where to Ask; The Kingdom of Heaven and 4th Dimensional Consciousness*, and *The Afterlife in the Here and Now*. These books take the reader up to and through the 6th Plane of Heaven.

Our Friday night class sessions included individual spiritual experiences, questions and answers, and discussions about related spiritual topics.

"In my teaching I believe the only solution to the mysteries of man's existence and of his toiling toward a goal he does not fully understand, is to seek the inner self. You cannot falter or fail in any way because you are beautiful, a living proof there is a God. Just know you are a channel for Christ's love to flow through." -- Mary Weddell

******

PART I

TEMPLES OF THE 7TH PLANE

MAP OF THE SEVENTH PLANE

THE SEVENTH PLANE OF HEAVEN
UNDER THE DIRECTION OF
THE HIERARCHY OF ST. GABRIEL

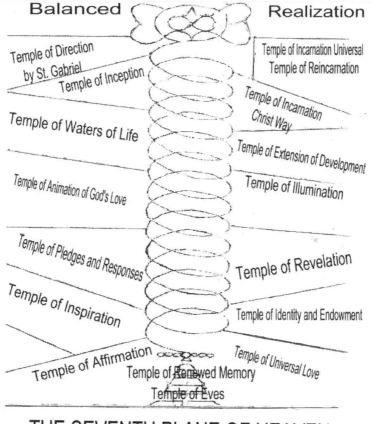

Balanced · Realization

Temple of Direction by St. Gabriel
Temple of Inception
Temple of Waters of Life
Temple of Animation of God's Love
Temple of Pledges and Responses
Temple of Inspiration
Temple of Affirmation

Temple of Incarnation Universal
Temple of Reincarnation
Temple of Incarnation Christ Way
Temple of Extension of Development
Temple of Illumination
Temple of Revelation
Temple of Identity and Endowment
Temple of Universal Love
Temple of Renewed Memory
Temple of Eves

THE SEVENTH PLANE OF HEAVEN

BEGINNING THE 7TH PLANE

Before beginning our adventures on the 7th Plane, we leave the Tower of the Soul, which is located on the Plateau between the 6th and 7th Planes. Encountering this temple in the fourth book of the Planes of Heaven series, *The Afterlife in the Here and Now: The 5th and 6th Planes of Heaven,* we were told:

"As time rolls on and age follows age, humanity's horizon grows brighter with added revelations of divine wisdom. The law of love is in an eternal state of unfoldment. Though the ordinary memory of man may not reach back to beginnings, the conscious soul may perceive its own past wanderings. Would you know the secret springs of human action, would you read the long history of lives past and present? Then look, for this night your eyes shall see truth, and your heart shall learn the law.

"When we entered this world of the soul, a new and strange picture was given us. We stood in awe as slowly a great veil parted until our eyes rested upon a glade. Before us it stretched into a forest of gigantic growth and dense foliage whose towering shrubs and gorgeous plants resembled nothing ever seen in books or travel. It was a tropical forest surrounding the Tower of the Soul. Even the birds and insects that flitted and hummed, and the serpents and lizards that glided and crawled through these emerald tints, were larger and more brilliantly colored than those with which the modern naturalist is familiar.

"Love opens the way into the garden of the soul, wherein God has planted a tree for every soul, whose fruits are intended for that soul alone. Pursuit of illumination is man's true nature. Listen with ears that hear. Does the bloom of a rose ever weary the eye or the song of a bird ever vex the ear? Does the perfect in nature ever pall either upon soul or sense? That which is allied by nature never separates, any more than the lily seeks divorce from the dewdrop or the sunflower asks separation from the sunlight.

"Your soul cannot be separated from God. Feel his presence in the crystal clearness of a lovely spring day, in the black spell of night when the moon sleeps behind the veil of shadows and the stars are like diamonds against a background of velvet. Beloved, flood your lives with Color, and live in the Tower of your Soul."

******

After leaving the Plateau between the 6th and 7th Planes we enter the 7th Plane. The 7th Plane is such an important plane in our lives. It touches a keynote as we go farther, touches certain planes that harmonize with it or that it supports as a foundation in our training. And you can watch for these things as we advance further and as you bring back a little more of your nighttime recollections.

The 7th Plane is where all previous tests are repeated in preparation for the 8th Plane and the Eightfold Path, where we will encounter "lions along the way," undesirable qualities needing to be cleared from our subconscious. The 7th is a plane of divine imagination, perseverance, and desire to share. We are conscious of truths learned and accepted while we were on the lower six planes, and now become aware that this new plane represents hidden life, the reality of unspoken thoughts, feelings and emotions.

The shape of the 7th Plane is a spiral, fourteen spirals becoming slightly smaller as they rise to the top. As we climb the right side of the spiral, we experience a résumé of our development and have tests to pass on each spiral. When we have looked into ourselves and can balance objectively, we will go down the left side, the side of future expectations.

Our life is reviewed before the august body of the Hierarchy. The teaching is personal; when you ask a question, you will always receive an answer. The teachers who reply know your life and can see the future. In every temple, we come out impressed with its silence, with a greater feeling that we can rid ourselves of stumbling blocks, and that by trading indifference for faith, we can remake our way and start rebuilding. Either you step in and go forward on this plane, or you do not advance further until you are up to the challenge.

MIRIAM WILLIS Adultship comes with 7th Plane. A 7th Plane person finds treasures of physical, mental, and spiritual health and guards them. No human soul can know security in this earth life, but there is security in the other life. As you reach a higher plane of awareness, remember that with it comes the challenge to live in that less dense atmosphere. The experience of deeper peace carries with it a profound realization of how life can be lived in emotional balance. Ask yourself this question: how much have I listened through the silence? What have I gained? What do I want?

BARBARA STONE Could what I experienced be a sense of moving to the next plane? I had a strong feeling of a subtle change. I couldn't put my finger on it; I had this feeling that we had made a step forward, but I didn't know what it was.

MARY We weren't quite ready for you to know you had reached the 7th Plane.

MIRIAM ALBPLANALP Did we all have to pass a particular test together? Because we seemed to be on the plateau preceding the 7th Plane for quite a long time while we were condensing ourselves into a unit.

MARY Your work on the Plateau between the 6th and 7th Planes was well done, or you couldn't have entered the 7th Plane.

GRACE HALE Mary, did you see me on the 7th Plane receiving help? I believe I brought back a special training, for I'm aware of being more balanced, and that I'm working more intensely in Creative Color; I feel more in rhythm with the Channel, and that I have recharged imagination by the application of color. I've proven how satisfying it is to pray in color, and to feel the healing presence as I pray.

MARY I will say this: each one of you this past week has worked on the 7th Plane. As you know, the 7th Plane is preparatory for the next plane and the Eightfold Path. We face tests here on Earth, and we account for them over there at night. Our real training here on the 7th Plane is in order to get firmly onto that Path and try harder to live in a developed way.

MIRIAM WILLIS So in the greater part of our training, we're going to keep working until you fully realize you're ready to enter the next phase, the Eightfold Path.

MARY This 7th Plane, as we've said, is the preparatory plane for the Eightfold Path, which to Buddhists is one of the most important teachings. The Essenes had it as man controlling himself using the three bodies. When we enter the Eightfold Path and we meet one "lion" after another, we know to conquer these lions along the way is really something.

WILLARD STONE Could you explain more what are these lions?

MIRIAM WILLIS They're dispositional qualities we don't want that we need to get rid of. We'll be talking about them more fully very soon.

LOLA GRUBE In meditation, I had a vision of a tall pagoda with seven roofs. I was below looking up at people at the top.

MARY That's seven steps.

JEANNE REJAUNIER Last night I also received something about seven. The latter part of my experience on the Other Side was a water test, in which I was told I had to bring seven friends along, and I understood that this meant seven qualities within myself.

MARY That's right.

RALPH MEEKS I had a vision in which I was like two different people, a lower self and a higher self. The lower self woke up before the higher self did, and I saw myself coming in on a spiral, getting back into the body.

MARY You have those 7th Plane spirals on your chart of the 7th Plane. That's where you were, returning from one of the spirals. You received enlarging vision. Keep track of everything. Your answer will come through.

EMILY On waking, I saw a flash of light, then a sheath of flowers, Canterbury bells, pink, blue and lavender ones all together.

MARY That's indicative of our colors on the 7th Plane.

ANDREW HOWE Is this a particular, special step because it's number 7? Seven is a mystical number. I was thinking about it this week, that there are "Orders of the Seven" in the heavenlies, and that connected in my mind to the 7th Plane.

PATTI CHALGREN I realize we don't go around actually delivering babies in our night work, but it seemed to me last night like we had done just that. Could that be symbolic? I brought that back upon waking. There were so many babies.

MARY Your influence of bringing the babies is the new birth you've come to as you made the change, this progression to the 7th Plane.

BARBARA In meditation and upon waking, I repeatedly saw a book bag loaded with heavy books. That came in several ways at different times, a total of seven times this past week. I was going to ask you what the meaning could be, and I wondered if it could have anything to do with the seven spiritual centers or the 7th Plane?

MARY It is. That's very good. The 7th Plane is a great deal like the 7th grade in school. Mathematics are getting harder, English demands more than before, you become almost – well, an adult, even in your thinking when you sit there and try to live up to what the teacher requires. Now I haven't been in school for a long time, but I've watched others, and I find that in seventh grade, their books become heavier, and most everything they bring home is just that much harder than it used to be.

MARGARET BRANCHFLOWER   Several times this past week, I saw the color of the 7th ray of the Spiritual Arc of Red, the color of salmon pink with the wide midray of deep rose.

MIRIAM WILLIS   This color is associated with the 7th Plane. Shall we add that its colors, deep rose and rose tinted with white light, are catalysts for change and development? Adding yellow to the rose creates the color of salmon pink, enlightens and lifts upward into spiritual life. The striped colors of this ray from right to left are: yellow-orange, rose, pastel rose, and pale yellow.

MARY   This ray reveals the source of supply to the aura. The orb within this ray can be either very pale yellow or rich sun yellow, according to the person's spiritual development. This is the ray we look for first when we read an aura, as it's the source of illumination to the aura. Its location also indicates the degree of development the person has attained.

MIRIAM WILLIS   We have many tests on the 7th Plane.

ANDREW HOWE   Does one of the tests take place where you're in a room all by yourself with nothing but light, and you feel it's more solemn than anything you've experienced for hundreds of years?

MARY   Indeed, a great loneliness overtakes us as we stand there, searching ourselves. At the foot of the Plane as you gaze upwards, you almost feel it's impossible to make it to the next rung, but somehow within you is born the thought that God will give you the power you need.

We took our tests at the prayer formation. Right there, you knelt and said that prayer which was the creative energy of all of you together. Each group creates their own prayer from the thoughts and the colors that are in them individually and together. The grandeur is something lovely to read. Putting into practice is something that can be a little difficult, but the simple prayer you prayed there was not so hard to fulfill.

We're climbing each day we live toward the next step up. Look at the chart, the map of the 7th Plane. As we climb up, we need a boost, and that's the reason that after a test, a teacher tells you you've passed it.

PATTI   A propos of the wonderful methods you use to help us, last night I brought back a brief fragment, the gist of which is: you can be magnetized in sleep so that you're lifted higher and higher, while the body remains still. The picture I received was like a wasp waist. You know how thin that wasp waist gets in the middle, as if the body were in two sections. The spiritual body being magnetized to rise is what I saw.

MARY   To me, the spiritual body is a sleeve within a sleeve, getting it down to a practical point in description. If it were magnetized, it could separate. That would be my description of it.

GENE HAFNER Usually I don't have any extra time in the morning, I just barely get to work in the nick of time, and sometimes I'm a little late. But today was different. I showed and shaved, and for some reason or other, I had plenty of time, so I sat down to write.

I wrote the question "What do I believe?" These then, are the things I answered: "Life is eternal; I am eternal. Earth is a school; we are here to learn lessons and have experiences; you can choose your own. The things that happen to us are not important, but how we react to them is. In other words, those are all tests. And we should react with no resentment, no jealousy, no hate, no retribution or envy or bitterness. No matter what happens to us, we should react with love, mercy, kindness, patience, understanding, and forgiveness."

MARY I think that's very wonderful.

******

THE TEMPLE OF RENEWED MEMORY

MIRIAM WILLIS Going straight up from the Plateau between the 6th and 7th Planes, the Tower of Life that leads us to the 7th Plane delivers us to the Temple of Renewed Memory.

MARY Here, we ask to be given the rites one experiences on entering the 7th Plane. Our prayer as we kneel on the first step is, "Oh Christ indwelling, give me knowledge of thyself in relation to my daily living. Feed my mind with thy living bread; give me the wisdom to know love conquers all things."

The path of the pilgrim can be full of light, for its darkness is of his own making. All man needs is to open the windows of his soul to divine truth and live in its greatness. If we will creative energy to shine through the human channel, mankind may come to understand the priceless gift and marvel at the harmony Christ's love can bring. For light can only change the darkness when we let it in; love can only change our dungeon when we clear it out. Light! God! They are the same.

MIRIAM WILLIS   We're climbing together into higher consciousness, each one contributing to the whole. Over and over again we receive the opening of our spirit, that we may be lured a bit farther and expand into yet higher consciousness. So as in the deep silence we share our powers, we give as well as receive.

MARY And this is free, a fluidic force we can walk with and live with. We who have walked together for quite some time in Color find the path gets harder the higher we climb. As we go into this Temple of Renewed Memory, we pass mirrors that reflect us as we are, as we were, and then in the end, as we grow in development, we clearly see what we are meant to be. That's the wonderful part.

You just seem to be always traveling toward this recognizable

19

goal. So the seeker is an eternal seeker. You go up before that mirror and you think, I thought I got over that fault, that problem, long ago. But here it is, it's still there; you see it. Where has it been hiding? You didn't want to see it again, so you just didn't see it. It slipped away, but it's there again.

LOLA This morning I woke with a recall of an experience last night in which I was climbing many steps going higher and higher. I was carrying a lovely child in my arms. When I got to the very top, there was an altar on which I laid this child. Maybe this is the Temple of Renewed Memory?

MARY It is. You did take the test for it, every one of you, and I'm happy to say you were well informed and you all answered without fear and with very little doubt. Some of you turned around and went back a few times, since you had to make up your minds whether you wanted to continue on. If we could go into our everyday life, it's the familiar things we want to stay with. But we must go on, we must borrow the building power, the energy to continue.

JANE WRIGHT I had an amazing experience in this temple. I believe this was a test which was combined with special training. I was required to balance an object that resembled a yellow tennis ball on my left palm. My eyes were simultaneously supposed to coordinate a series of numbers that appeared every few seconds on the upper area of the same palm. These numbers were small, difficult to read, and changed every time the ball bounced on the opposite end of my palm. Each time the ball bounced, I was asked to recite the fast changing numbers, which consisted of a string of about ten or twelve digits. This was a real feat to accomplish.

It was partly a hand/eye coordination exercise, but it was actually more than that. It was training the mind, my quickness of thought. No way in the physical world could I possibly have executed an exercise like this, but in the spiritual body, it was perfectly natural. All that was needed was my cooperation, my total focus and the faith that I could do it. I believe this was training me to be able to think on my feet, to be better able to make quick decisions in my physical life, and that it was also a test. It was just incredible!

MARY It was indeed a test, and everyone in the class was tested in a similar manner. Thank you, Jane, for telling us.

*****

THE TEMPLE OF UNIVERSAL LOVE

The Temple of Universal Love is the first temple on the right hand side of the 7th Plane.

Color is the handmaiden of Universal Love. It is in your attitudes; it is the thought of God in moments when you're alone. Faith carries you beyond the doorway of the material plane through the Channel of Color until you can prove the invisible becomes visible, and the transmutation of all your development has become power motivated only by love.

MIRIAM WILLIS To Mary, the Temple of Universal Love is the most beautiful of any temple.

MARY When you go into this temple, you think, "Whom have I loved most?" As you look at the wall and wonder if someone knows how much you love them, you see their name and picture appear on the wall. You learn how many people feel kindly toward you. Hatred and indifference can't exist in this temple. When you see people hovering at the entrance and quickly leaving, you know they've not shared as they should; they took more than they were willing to give.

Alone in the Temple of Universal Love, man sings only the untutored strains of his heart, a hymn unuttered by any other voice. Color endows him with rare wild blossoms that grow spontaneously on the highest tracts of his soul. From this temple, we receive a new formula to live by, and understand that we can, through love, realize particular gifts: first, vision of purpose; second, the desire to live through creative power, and third, to know that by faith universal love can happen to all men.

Seven lights are given us in this temple: the light of intelligence, of truth, color, faith, personality, wisdom, and love. And we see seven reflected lights: the light of the sun, the light of fire, a consuming light; then a radiant light shines forth on the seeds of divinity. In their beginning they are very small, bright scintillating lights. We each offer to God the theme that our heart chants secretly. Consciousness is the ego's powerhouse. I ask for this class that the lonely, separately moving streamlets of their affections merge in a lake of unlimited love, that the narrow rivers of their lives be widened by torrential rains of blessings as they enter in purity the blissful sea.

MARGARET In the Temple of Universal Love, I affirmed the right to live in this universal way. I received information from the teachers that my will was granted to me for the purpose of being who I am, expressing the best that I am, that my free will enables me to make choices that define my path in life. I went forward, singing this song of universal love which is my own song.

HELEN MARSH From this temple, I brought back the image of a solid, five foot tall curving jade wall with three rows of carving that was either ancient Babylonian or Egyptian. Seeing this upon waking, I felt free and absolutely wonderful.

PATTI Last night I saw our class arriving on the Other Side at "Grand Central Station." Other groups were gathered there as well. Many men and women were in clothes of different periods in history, and they moved about just as we do when we go out. From what I saw, these people seemed to glide like dynaflow or automatic shift or something like that. Each of them was on that gliding force.

But the strange thing is that they were not going in tandem, one after another. They were each isolated one from another, separate on this force that moved them, and each was going in different directions, but nobody hit one another. It was as if coordinated. Could you explain?

MARY Perfect rhythm and order. When we have a thought of that other world, it seems that chemistry is the only word you can use to describe the order in the Heaven World. Matchless things come up there. Rhythm, gliding – it never ceases. And it all seems to be so filled with creativity that carries with it the flowing light of understanding. You know what it is when you see it, yet you couldn't possibly describe it here. I have not the words to describe some of the beauty I see over there.

As we're taken into the temples, we see their colored fountains, we see the beautiful plumage on birds. You see a great deal of flowering trees. Those flowers and trees are so different, so vibrant. Matchless beauty. We come back to this life, and we see that what we have on Earth has been patterned after that world. Then, as we think of the movement of dawn breaking into the high sun of noon, going into the sunset, back into the dark of night, we live in that same rhythm, but we don't recognize it. It's going beyond anything that anyone can describe.

MIRIAM WILLIS Mary has had a certain experience repeatedly over there: she has nicked off a fruit, eaten it, and had it disappear. She has picked a flower and worn it, and as she took that flower off a bush, another one instantly appeared. The world of heaven is a magical place. "And no man shall be blind; the blind shall see."

DALE COPE Speaking of blindness, I know that even blind people can have a sense of color. Helen Keller, who was blind, for instance, said she saw color and even described what she "saw." I was wondering, Mary, have you had colorblind people in your classes who saw color, or anybody who was actually totally blind who experienced color?

MARY Colorblind people who saw color, yes, many. And as for the totally blind, I had one such blind person in my Color class who positively saw light. Because I myself could see auras, I asked if he could read auras. He would hold the person's hand, put his face against the other person's for the vibratory activity of the two minds. He was in a wheelchair, way in his 70's when he took the Color course. He had sight and hearing — and gave me one of the biggest pieces of advice I ever received from anyone.

One day he just simply said, "I see in your aura," and then he told me what was the matter with me. He said, "You're very anemic and you're not recognizing it." I thanked him. I hadn't thought about the possibility that I was anemic, but I went to the laboratories to find out, and I was. It wasn't even secondary anemia. In that year I had eleven transfusions. That was the blind man: he said he knew it from the first time he ever touched my hand.

Many people said to him, "Will you talk to me and let me write a book about you?" He said, "The Book of Life will be opened. I do not expect to do great things while I'm here, because I'm a burden to whomever has to care for me. Therefore, I shall wait until I get to the Other Side, and then some brilliant young person will want to write that book. And if they're clean enough and dear enough, I will help them write it!"

PATTI   We were talking about Grand Central Station. Are the other people we see at Grand Central Station brought there by teachers who, like Mary Weddell, are in the physical body?

MARY   Yes. Grand Central Station is where people who work in the temples meet. It's a teeming mass of people that all seems so orderly. They're all nationalities, all colors and all races.

GENE   Mary, the approach that you take when we go over across, I suppose there are other teachers who take different approaches, and maybe go other places than we do. Do lots of different activities go on at the same time?

MARY   Yes indeed. We're just one small group. We're just one in the midst of them all. We follow a Color path which is safe. We have an accumulated knowledge of devoted people who believe in Christ and the manifestation of the works he did. We believe that he perfected the human life, that he left us a path to follow that shows us the way we can perfect our lives, as he did.

HELEN MARSH   When anyone speaks of "Grand Central

Station," I receive a vision of a broad path, always a large building in back of me. I see temples. It' s a wonderful feeling.

MARY Well, just embrace it, because the temples will be given you, and the description of them comes through that vibratory rate of your thinking. In other words, we become accustomed to bringing things through, and after a little while it's always there for us.

ANDREW Do you ever see people living up to what they're given over there?

MARY Yes, I do. I see people not only living up to but even beyond what you'd expect. I also see people pushing themselves too hard trying, having created a duty that's heavy to carry. Through development, these people will find there's another way of shifting the burden so they won't have to carry such a load. Under development, we can't be burdened and still walk lightly or ride light in the saddle. We simply must have freedom.

GENE   I know night travel to the heaven world is safe and protected, but have you ever had a student who couldn't tolerate this path of spiritual work and rejected it?

MARY A student of ours, every time he came to our Friday night class, would have this dream of a storm at sea, and he'd become terribly disturbed. I would take him out, but he would go back to the Sleep World. I have no control over a person if they want to go back; it's entirely up to them.

RALPH What happens to the spiritual development of someone like that?

MARY Some people don't care to go on. We see things in ourselves we don't like. Anyone who has a desire to withdraw will never lose what they gained. It's a love tie that can't be broken, yet you're not bound to this or indeed to any teaching. You always have a choice. Sometimes people will stagnate or find something else that's more of an adventure for them. Then they should certainly be released for that adventure, to follow another path.

******

THE TEMPLE OF AFFIRMATION

Opposite the Temple of Universal Love, we enter the Temple of Affirmation. After a silence we seem to awaken as from a deep refreshing sleep. We are led to look out of a crystal window and see the receding stars pull down the curtains of their chambers and retire to rest. We stand erect, throw back our shoulders, and by a process of thought, let the winds of this sphere wash our faces clean, cause our thoughts to be reburnished, and in the golden mist of God's love, the imprint of universal power again illumines the surface of our souls.

After partaking of communion in this temple, we call to our sides those friends whom we love; then, clad in the long robes of our individual colors, we affirm our vows. We walk down a long aisle. An instrument sounding like a great organ fills the vast hall to its foundations with sharp, staccato chords; then vibrations change and the music is played in yet more intense color. Through the temple's large windows appear varied hues, beautiful as the most gorgeous life in the tropical regions on the earth plane.

We don't sit down. Standing at ease, swaying back and forth, we keep time breathing to the strains of the music and the vibrations of the tinted light as it flows from the temple windows. At a given signal, we stop breathing for a fraction of time, so to concentrate our attention on a speaker at the rostrum. Then in unison more perfect than was ever expressed by the musicians on earth, we breathe deeply and drink in the inspiration of the Master's teaching.

As the vast jasper-like doors of the temple move back, white filmy tapestries are pulled down over the great windows. Like glowworms of our forests whose phosphorescent beauty is caught from the love light of angels' eyes, this pale pink twilight lowers and dims until it becomes a strange, weird radiance which soothes our very souls.

MARY Quite a number of you have met up with doors lately. I noticed as you were going through tests, you were asked: have you entered an open door? Some of you said yes, you had seen the door open. Others said no, I haven't entered it yet ... should I, when I come to it again? Kindly, the teachers answered yes.

PATTI I saw a door with four panels. The door was lavender except in the center panel, where there were four dots of pale yellow-green.

ANDREW I saw an arch-shaped entrance with double doors. Outside in the courtyard, I saw a group of people clad in pale lavender centered around a brilliant orb of light. This was a power center for bringing our consciousness up. Entering the temple through these double doors, you see a place of worship with an altar. There's a central aisle with seats on either side. In a smaller room inside the temple, we were shown pictures that revealed where we're lacking. We were then shown what we can do about our weaknesses.

GRACE I've had this same particular recurring dream many times. I'd be so surprised to open a door and realize I didn't know I had this room in my house.

MIRIAM WILLIS Many of us have had similar dreams, Grace.

ESTHER BARNES To me, when I have a dream like Grace is describing, it means I'm discovering spiritual truths I didn't know before.

BARBARA I saw a shrine in cranberry red. There were candles with gold filigree. I felt the presence of the Buddha. I went through a white cross that was a door, then I was inside a cave that was like an enormous gold nugget. Classes were held there.

MIRIAM WILLIS Heaven is a great ordered place. A real seeker is never denied that door to enter.

MARY   It's affirmed in this temple that we have a greatness we don't recognize when we're walking about in our daily life. In the Temple of Affirmation, we affirmed the fact that we wanted all the knowledge that could be given us. We realized ever more how if you find yourself repeating old habits, do away with the detrimental ones, break those old molds and make new, better habits.

Within this temple is the Order of the Single Eye. "If thine eye be single ..." That is affirmed here. Keep focused on that single eye. This is a time of absorption of the rhythms of life, color, and music, all of which are contained in our lessons in the Temple of Affirmation. This life ray surrounding all is the vitality of togetherness with the work at night. We realize the great silence of generative love and peace lies within as a source to be drawn upon whenever needed. It is not the mental processes we use, but wisdom from the hidden spiritual source of the Christ teaching, through the listening, obedient heart.

JANE   I had a profound experience in the Temple of Affirmation which I believe related both to fear and also to my personal dislikes. It may have been a test; it certainly was instructive. It started with the sight of a very ugly small insect that at first I couldn't identify, but which soon became what I recognized as a cockroach. Since I intensely dislike cockroaches, I was immediately repelled.

But no sooner did I express disgust than the horrid cockroach started growing and enlarging, becoming even more repugnant. It acquired much longer legs and a rapidly increasing larger body. It just kept expanding and expanding, and I was helpless to know what to do, as it was only a few inches from me and I found it so repulsive and scary.

Very soon, what had started out as a small bug turned into the proportions of a medium size dog, around the size of a cocker spaniel, and it was no longer a bug but had become a mammal that retained the ugly brown color of the original bug. Remembering its origins, I couldn't overcome my feelings of revulsion for the mammal, whatever species it was. I quickly went to the door and issued it out, wanting only to be rid of it.

Later, I thought how the creature this bug turned into was actually sweet and adorable, that it might have been a labradoodle, which is a type of dog I really like, but I had immediately rejected it without allowing myself to appreciate its friendly and attractive qualities. Had I not had the experience of the bug/ cockroach, had I not had the original fear and disgust, had I encountered this brown mammal/labradoodle with no prior history, I would have immediately liked and welcomed such a sweet and lovely warm blooded creature.

The experience was very telling to me about prejudice, close mindedness, and fear. It certainly gave me pause to examine myself. Upon reflection, I knew that I had affirmed in this temple a resolve to work on my hidden prejudices and judgments. What a deep, meaningful experience of self-revelation! I woke with a sense of gratitude, having understood much that was previously unknown to me. I want to say that this was one of the most meaningful experiences I have ever had in our night work on the Other   Side.

******

THE TEMPLE OF IDENTITY AND ENDOWMENT

As we enter the temple, we see in shining letters: "The Universe is God." This is our first premise, based on extensive empirical thought in the chambers of concentration, that God, the Universe, is really one great, all comprehensive soul-mind, divided into three divisional strata: the passive, physical world; the great area of imagination; and the serene, rare, pure inspirational center of God intelligence.

After the physical consciousness in its infinitely varied manifestations reaches a higher degree of development, we then enter the field of divine imagination.

MARY   In the Temple of Identity and Endowment, we're made to see every thought, action and nuance of our ego. This is the realm of pure vision, imagination, and picture life, primarily where the seeing of every thought and action of one's own ego is as it concerns in the most infinitesimal detail the ego of another. This is the true beginning of divine unfoldment, because it reveals to the ego endless vistas of roads to traverse to gain the high road of consciousness.

The entire Spiritual Arc of Blue, "Training of the Ego," is important in this temple, and much emphasis is placed on its twelve color rays.

MIRIAM WILLIS As in our meditations, we're climbing together into higher consciousness, each of us contributing to the whole. Over and over again, we revive our thinking process and the opening of our spirit that we may be lured a bit farther and expand into a yet higher consciousness. So in the deep silence we share our powers. Here the seeker learns to combine his forces in unity of purpose. Here he identifies himself.

MARY   The Temple of Identity and Endowment has but one floor, but the roof is so high we can't see it, hence some have called this a roofless temple, although at some point after a time, some start to perceive a frosted glass ceiling in the main hall.

Identity and Endowment has to do with what we were given when we came into the world, the gifts we start out with in this life. You have no conception of the things you're going to hear in this temple. If you made the 7th Plane and come to this temple, you've been endowed with a certain identity that will be with you for the rest of your life. We were surprised to learn what we discovered here.

MIRIAM WILLIS Besides being considered a roofless temple, the main entrance of the Temple of Identity and Endowment has no door. On steps of variegated colors, anyone may pass immediately to the heart of the temple. One glides rather than walks as we enter a circular area of pink lavender alabaster. The floor looks like pure clear water that is flashing with colors from deep aqua to light turquoise and palest green. Many fountains are playing in rainbow colors, casting rays of varying hues from the central fountain. Moving about, one encounters walls of onyx and jasper and sixty large French windows draped with magnificent tapestries. There are many smaller rooms, places of soul-rest; bedrooms with beds whose covers are soft quilts of silk that could be pulled through a ring. The average temperature here is 110 degrees Fahrenheit. You will ask, would such a temperature enervate?

ANDREW How could you possibly determine the temperature?

MARY   We were told that the temperature there is just that, and that those who come here are created equal to that temperature, just like some plants grow in the sun and some in the shade. In class, I sometimes say, it's getting so warm in here the teachers from the other side can't stay with us. Over there, it's the same thing. Those who dwell there are created equal to that temperature. It's altogether a case of pre-development. No soul could reach this plane that would fall back.

We have substantial shrines of art here. One room is called the Inspiration Room. In this room hang pictures painted in words expressly for each person, a moving picture of dreams on the wall. The walls are made of glass, and as one dreams, the life is pictured on the wall as mural decoration, a moving picture of the tenants. We sometimes sweep out articles and slowly create new things of beauty, such as beds shaped like golden sands heated by the intense sun. We have rugs something like a blend of fur, silk, and cashmere.

This temple has great beauty and many teachers work here. It's the one temple that you truly feel you belong in. Everywhere you look you're made to feel at home. With all the beauty and elegance around you, we come back to a simplicity that is shared by everyone. You notice long draperies that are weightless. The comfort you feel is colossal; that's the only word that expresses it.

I thought, where have I felt anything like this? I remembered my first down quilt after I had been to this temple. My mother got out some down quilts and made them smaller so we could each have one. She gave them to each of us for Christmas. I carried back to the temple the softness, the ease. There's no weight anywhere in this temple. Everything is weightless. You cannot describe the chiffons and the elegance of tapestries because you haven't the words. But they hang in rich folds, as light as a feather. I have deliberately gone over and lifted one of those long draperies out of curiosity. It weighed nothing.

People change clothing here ... they see some color in the tapestry that appeals to them, and before you know it, they have put that on and are wearing it. This temple is such a creative place. I'm trying to give you a picture of how creative you become while in this temple. It's all simplicity, nothing ornate, but there's an elegance beyond expression here.

The power we receive here: we are endowed with an understanding of the right of identity. We've asked for it, we have accepted it. It has been given us freely. What are you going to do with it? You can have imagination here if you never had any before. All you have to do is to lift into it.

EMILY   In my dream, I was creating a dress out of materials, some new and some old. It wasn't looking good when I finished it. But then it changed for much the better. Singing was flowing through me, words and melody. I was endowed with music.

MARY When you were endowed with music you also were given the thought that all the old should be left behind. Each one of us, as we entered that temple, was told to leave old things behind, that there was an endowment here that we were to receive.

WILLARD I recalled a ceremony. I was taken to a four poster bed with a canopy. I remember lovely green hangings softer than cushions.

SYLVIA HOWE   I think if we had all gone to the Temple of

Identity and Endowment, that we'd all feel differently and have a different view of ourselves, considering the uniqueness of everyone.

MARY   Among the many things that were asked that night, nothing was denied. But we have to learn to ask in order to receive. We take too much for granted. There is that in the ego of man that he doesn't want to be subservient to others. We're subservient to no one but God. The glorification of Christ's life is given us many times in this temple. The teachers would like to have us go the entire breadth of the area of the temple before we forget, in order that the temple should stay with us.

******

THE TEMPLE OF INSPIRATION

MARY In attempting to reveal to you the beauty and simplicity of the unfoldment which has been going on since this work at night on the heavenly planes has opened up new vistas of consciousness, I've attempted to describe these many temples, trying to awaken the joyful, thrilling spirit of the quest.

As we enter this Temple of Inspiration, we find our heads involuntarily bowing in thankfulness for the wonder of it all, or a casting of our eyes in a quick upward glance of gratitude to the great giver of life. In each place in this temple where we meet in worship, the music of a magnificent organ is played to arouse the music in one's soul. The tunes played seem to give a clue to the words being sung. But one of the most pleasurable features of these services is that between every verse of every hymn, the master at the organ lets the fancy of his genius wander away into the happiest and most brilliant of improvisations, sometimes on the theme of the hymn, but as often where inspiration leads him, which always leads him and us closer and closer to the throne of God.

On leaving the temple, we walked into a stretch of savannah-meadows; then entering a deep forest, we wandered along rivers, and eventually we were beside a calm and peaceful lake. Each of us stood by our own tree; we had each been inspired by that tree.

As we moved on, the scene changed; all over the sky there had drawn what looked like a thin, light mist. As we watched, it solidified and became like a huge frosted mirror. And on this mighty mirror there suddenly flamed out the mystic wonder of the aurora borealis shooting up hither and thither, forked fingers of delicate multi-colored flames pulsing like the beats of a mighty heart, bewildering and breathless in their ceaseless activities.

Presently the scene changed again, and on the frosted mirror appeared a slender finger tracing a design of fascinating beauty. It swept all over and around us in masterful rolls and scrolls until the whole face of the mirror was covered with beauties beyond telling. And in the channels thus marked, out rushed a stream of life of every color one had ever dreamed of or seen: a clear crystalline green, yellow, red, blue, orange, and gold – all leaping, sparkling, alive with the music of Christ's life. And inherent in it all and flowing out from it was an undertone of holy music—soft and uplifting, that seemed to bind the whole picture together.

As we left the temple we joined a procession of people clad in shining white robes, their faces glowing with the joy of life and love. Suddenly the music died away, the procession stopped, and there fell upon all a great expectant silence so profound it seemed as though the whole universe were straining every nerve to catch what was coming.

Then we heard the Voice—calm, quiet, majestic, going right into the heart of every soul in that vast multitude, thrilling every being to the core. Said the Mighty: "These are they who have served me well. My heart rejoices in them."

MIRIAM WILLIS The Temple of Inspiration fills the soul with a power that presses to be born. Its predominant colors are pale coral rose and pale olive. We perceive how forms of inspiration grow in maturity and clarity.

MARGARET   Miriam's mention of pale coral rose is meaningful to me because that coral rose, the 6th ray of the Spiritual Arc of Red, the meaning of which is clear thinking and pure purpose, is my keynote color. I've found in this color such joy and help. It's much needed in so many ways, one of which is stabilizing me, gathering and organizing my thoughts, helping me to understand what is most important.

MARY Added power for this color comes in the Temple of Inspiration.

HELEN VON GEHR There are Temples of Inspiration on lower planes and higher planes. Each succeeding plane is a higher octave with higher responsibilities and responses.

ANDREW When we're going out at night visiting the temples, what is the main thing we should remember before we go?

MARY Pray before sleeping. There must be thought or a connection made between pupil and teacher. If you want to go out at night, pray. Unless you're connected, you can't be picked up.

MIRIAM WILLIS Be glad that we walk and talk in rhythm, that we have such privileges. We should come back with a kindness in our heart toward the teachers who have given their time over there.

BARBARA I'm so happy to be able to see my sister these nights on the Other Side. I know there must be many people who wish they were so blessed. Why are some people able to visit with loved ones who've passed on as I can, and others never seem to be able to?

ESTHER BARNES Wouldn't that have something to do with knowing and believing you can see your loved one, whereas many people just don't know or believe they can?

FRED ADLER Sunday and Tuesday nights, we have special family nights for these occasions when we see our loved ones over there, and we can see them at other times, too. But some people have no interest in that; some people don't care to see their loved ones.

MARY If you don't love anyone enough to see them, you will not see them. If you do want to speak to a certain person, you go to an "information bureau" and ask for them. After a certain time, a date will be set, then you'll initially meet in a great hall, probably. After that it's not so complicated if you want to meet again. The people on the Other Side love to see us. Love is always expressed. If there's anyone you want to thank on that side, this is a good time.

PATTI You mentioned that when we go out at night and see our loved ones on the Other Side, we're told by the teachers not exactly what we can say but how we should say it.

MARY Yes, Patti. We are emotional. Well, that world is not a world of emotion; it's a world of balance. And so we're told how to speak and keep the vibration in balance between the two of us. And we're told never to express negativity.

For instance, one of my students, we'll call her Paula, wanted to see her mother on the Other Side. Paula hadn't spoken to her sister in five years; the sister had gone over after the mother. Well, Paula was absolutely adamant she wanted to see her mother but definitely not her sister. And suddenly she found herself back in her bed with a thud. The next day she phoned me. She didn't want to believe what happened. And I said, "Think that you go into that world carrying spite with you!" She got the point.

*****

THE TEMPLE OF REVELATION

MIRIAM WILLIS One approaches this temple through a beautiful garden of multi-colored flowers, flowering shrubs and fruit trees. To the neophyte, these reveal qualities of fragrance and exquisite loveliness beyond anything before experienced, because the infilling of inspiration has awakened a keenness of heightened enlightenment. As one glides along the paths admiring the flowers, partaking of the nectar of the fruit, the fruit and flowers appear in all their beauty. The nectar is pungent with a delicate fragrance as well as the rarest flavor and refreshing reality.

The temple is a vast many turreted edifice of translucent amethyst, soft purples, pinks and lavender to almost white. Its pinnacles reach into the sky above and seem to disappear beyond one's vision. Within are many chambers extending outward from a large central foyer.

These chambers are diffused with a strange light that reveals in a slowly moving picture growing forms of the inspirations received in that temple. They mature according to the depth and reality of the inspiration, and grow in clarity and maturity as one identifies with the revealed. This is recreated until one has grown to the degree necessary to perfect the revelation through expression in this earth life.

LOLA Miriam's description makes me think of what I saw during our meditation tonight. I saw a temple; I felt it was like the mirror you can see out from – you know, the black mirrors you can see out of and no one can see in. It was purple. It was very tall and about half way up, there was a ring of white sort of cumulus clouds, and then it went on tapering and tapering into more clouds.

MARY That was an oval temple?

LOLA I thought it was.

MARY And its revealing is growth from that temple; all our growth is revealed to us. We're aware in this temple that life is an unending revelation, that the law of life is progress, a procession to the divine. And as all movement carries with it a certain zest, the sternness of the law changes into the joy of life.

Laughter becomes the sunlight of the spirit, lightening the burden of man's existence and his sorrow-darkened spirit. Tears are indeed a divine gift. They are a talisman for learning the secrets of the self. Silence of spirit is the best of prayers. It's a vision and a whisper of the eternal, the infinite, a divine glimpse of the universe as a living and luminous habitation. Light is God's language; it's the language of recognition and relationship. Hence, man's age long prayer, "Light, more light."

Light is the signature and seal of the divine. Love is the rainbow fashioned out of a fusion of tears and smiles, of self sacrifice and self unfoldment. Clear before us lies the path of revelation, where the soul absorbs into itself all that is beautiful and true and gives it back to God. In this constant process of interpenetrating power passing back and forth between God and the individual soul, development follows. Man then knows and has revealed to him God's plan for his life.

As the sun is obscured by clouds, so often this plan is hidden from man's sight. Growth is advancement toward wholeness. A life attuned to walk on this path of revelation becomes accustomed to the action of divinity upon it, in that it is finally the natural state of that life, rather than the miraculous or unusual.

MICHAEL Your mentioning the sun being obscured by clouds reminds me that in the spiritual traditions of India, consciousness is understood as being obscured by defilements which are compared to clouds covering the sun. These defilements are accumulations in the unconscious caused by past actions. Because of them, what one perceives as reality is a picture of the world filtered through one's unconscious conditioning.

The goal is to awaken, to dissolve delusion to effect transformation. Enlightenment enables us to see reality as it is, rather than through the veils of Maya. We open ourselves to the indwelling spirit. Every man has God within, a direct celestial ray from the Absolute, whether you call it God, Yahweh, Jehovah, Allah, the Logos, the Elohim, or any other names that transcends the power of human conception and is beyond human thought.

VIOLET STEVENS As I entered the 7th Plane Temple of Revelation, I noticed a number of pendant crystals forming columns four feet square each. Aisles off to the sides displayed crystals and flowers. The whole interior radiated this and there were rays of color everywhere. The central part of the temple was like the long nave of great cathedral. At the far end is a colored fountain. One walks around the fountain. We were each wrapped in our own keynote color, which became clearer and clearer as we were cleansed and enlightened.

HELEN MARSH   Waiting inside the temple, I noticed that the wall curved, and around it was a seat with a high back in the colors of lettuce green of compassion, the rose color of love, and sapphire blue, the color of moral courage, as in the side rays of the 5th psychological ray of blue. As it was my turn to move up, I saw an angel take off and fly high up.

MARY I think you were being called. We usually are called that way. It's something that you've been asking yourself for quite some time. You've been trying to remember and trying to account for something that took place in your life that bothered you; you wonder now why it bothered you so much. And it was revealed to you last night, through the mirrors—just the whole reaction as you would see a movie. So you had a revelation, you have gone to the Temple of Revelation and seen what's recorded there, so that was a starting point of a new life. You had that experience. You'll recall it.

VIOLET In the Temple of Revelation is there a special emphasis on pride?

MARY Well, yes; pride is a barrier to the development of the human soul.

MARGARET After preliminary symbols were given me, I waited, knowing more was to come. I'm shown pictures, but I don't realize they're pictures until it's all finished. Misty layers form. There's a faint golden rosy glow from the setting sun. Always the great giver of life watches over us, feeding us what we need for spiritual growth.

JEANNE   Along the way to the temple, I saw several very impressive and dramatic purple geysers, each about thirty feet high. I approached the Temple of Revelation, which appeared first as amethyst, purple and lavender to a darkened silver, then a paler silver melding into white. At the top of a winding staircase we met the highest part of the teaching. You go into a small room where alone with the infinite, the revelation given is enlightenment that you realize could be yours, with a knowledge within of your unrealized but realizable potential. You know that only your own willfulness keeps you from expanding into that greater consciousness.

I recall being in a development room. Here, a voice tells us our capacity and shows the plan that is ours. There are many small rooms where we go for reckoning. We were asked questions like: what did you do with the supply you were blessed with, and what did you do for others with your supply? You're told to look for your positive credits and that you would be astonished to find how much you've done for others.

LOLA   As I knelt at an altar, I perceived that purple light as if carved from rock was enveloping me. I turned into a corridor, then another one, and climbed a spiral stairway going up to a tower. Here I stood in front of onyx mirrors where all that has become my own along the Path was revealed. I next went out on a balcony that offered a view of a beautiful valley, where I   envisioned expectations for development that need yet to be fulfilled.

HELEN DE CANT   I saw Doric columns fronting an archway covered with gold and opalescent fish scales, then a hallway in dimmed light. I became aware of a teaching that was meaningful to me: when you see a fault in another person, you know that you either were once where that person is, or you're still there yourself, and you need to overcome that fault.

VIOLET I entered many rooms. Each one was filled with unusual forms and objects made of wood like a nut wood that represented the hard things in life. We have to break through that hard nut and arrive at something more edible. In these rooms, people were able to make changes in the structure. If one took a hard wood ball, it turned into an edible fruit.

HELEN VON GEHR I brought back a fountain with a center pole of lettuce green, the color of compassion, and the 12th ray of the Spiritual Arc of Green, at-one-ment with God. There was a dove perched on top. One flower after another, each in shades of pink and lavender, was brought into bloom.

MIRIAM WILLIS   Many of us were also deeply affected in this temple by the 10th ray of the Spiritual Arc of Green, that beautiful, soft sea foam green that symbolizes the awareness of sowing and reaping, the law of compensation – as ye sow, so shall ye reap. This ray, of which we need be ever mindful, signifies the relentless rhythm of the ocean tides and reminds us that what comes in must go out, where there is cause there is effect.

LINDA CLARK What goes around comes around. Karma.

MIRIAM WILLIS   This ray helps the seeker to be alert and receptive to the inflowing currents of soul wisdom to replace his ego-centered concepts. The 10th ray of spiritual green is a balancing ray that encourages growth that constantly challenges one to new goals and helps us recognize unrewarding patterns.

MARY Every year that you're in this work you need a little more proof. You need to get that proof yourself. Break the old molds. Recreate the thinking process so that everything is enlightened. That's why we're in Color. That's why the Planes are given to us.

*****

THE TEMPLE OF PLEDGES AND RESPONSES

As we neared the Temple of Pledges and Responses, we watched a golden cloud of prayers rising into the ethers. On an ascending scale, individual prayers rose from earth to the planes of spirit filled with love of God substance.

We then crossed a silver river over a bridge of blue and came to a building four-square made of white marble blocks. This stadium like building seats many thousands. Many people were there wearing different colors. We knew their chosen line of service by the colors in the garment each wore as a badge of distinction.

Looking around with interest, to our amazement we saw a great host of brothers wearing the colors of the Order of St. John. We knew by the radiance of their colors that they were well advanced in the Essene teaching. We were deeply grateful to be numbered among them. They rayed out their brilliance to us until we were enveloped in all shades of the purples.

Our teachers took us into the lecture room where we were given a vision of expansion of consciousness. Later we found ourselves in a cubicle where our earthly experiences rolled before our view. We fully recognized each experience. After reviewing for some time our achievements and failures, we vowed we would try to overcome, to fulfill through eternal prayer our eternal lives.

Soon strains of music to which we had been listening were caught up and amplified by angelic voices overhead. Slowly the lights in the center began to change. It's impossible for earth minds to conceive the colors of the heavenly lights. Raising our eyes to the radiant peak of a mountain before us, we realized the glowing beauty of its glorious crown of Christ blue, which began in soft, billowing, cloudlike films of light over the entire ceiling of heaven's dome.

At first we beheld only the basic white brilliance of spiritual light. Slowly it changed to living gold with ruby lights of great beauty. We had all been instructed in the meaning of the colors and intensity of brilliance. We were told to always recognize this combination as Christ's love in action. With this color man overcomes his faults and the sin of separation from God. When the gold light was rayed on us, we recalled glad manifestations of the spiritual gains we have made in this life on earth. Joyously we pledged our allegiance to God and man and came back to serve to the best of our capacity.

MIRIAM WILLIS   We approach the Temple of Pledges and

Responses through a forest of thick evergreens. One must hunt his way through. As he does so, he finds an energy coursing through his being. A light shines on his path, spanning sparkling blue water, until his eyes alight on a temple four-square, rectangular, massive and very strong, of hand hewn marble. The temple seems to have no door. Within, the soft silvery light is alive against the walls of red purple.

There are many antechambers, and one is drawn to one's own. Entering, he is clothed in his keynote color and hears his own keynote. Gradually he sees his destiny. As he accepts it, the plan becomes clearer to his understanding and he draws a mantle of faith over himself.

VIOLET   So suddenly does this temple loom up before us that we're taken by surprise. We have climbed quite a hill to get here, amongst tall trees and other vegetation all about. Now we see it, the massive pile of white stone of heavy seeming blocks, pleasing lines and no windows.

The whole interior gives the impression of velvet, as if it were overlaid with rich designs of large flowers in various colors, giving the effect of a subdued texture. Each silently entered a cubicle. The room I went into was decorated in all shades of blue. The realization came that one could carry out what they were intended to do.

BARBARA   When we enter the Temple of Pledges and Responses, we acknowledge the pledges we've given on the way up. Some people forgive themselves for their lack of awareness. In this forgiveness, they become energized in new thought and new life. The equipment was always there for them to work things out, but they were their own block.

We declare the pledges and responses we're making in our lives from now on to God and to ourselves. For the first time, we realize we're not alone, but with our classmates.

MARY   The music we heard was beyond words to express. Next, we heard the deep and solemn Voice utter sixteen words: "Unto you who have given your vows and pledges, may you find enlightenment in God's will."

******

THE TEMPLE OF ILLUMINATION

MARY At the Temple of Illumination, each soul in its course of development is given a spiritual vision and finds itself in a blissful state. Yet there is something about this vision that seems a warning. We are aware that we alone are responsible to become the enlightened being we were viewing. One should, at this temple, not only remember his experience but also realize he has expanded in spiritual consciousness, and from that time on should enjoy daily life more than ever before by continuing to demonstrate the spiritual truths given in night work in the temples.

One learns all natural phenomena are but the shadows of the spirit from which they spring. He knows color in nature washes in its warm waves of vibration, showing in vision what spiritual love would do if once let loose in the world. This vision seems to extend through all laws, all knowledge, all science, all history, and all religion. He senses that all through nature the grand rhythms roll, and that heaven and earth are filled with melody.

The soul who truly benefits from this temple experience is the soul that ascends to the mesa of God consciousness, for the soul's union with God is illumination. The visible world is sustained by the invisible. So cherish your visions, your ideals; cherish the music that stirs in your heart, the beauty that forms in your mind, the loveliness that drapes your purest thoughts, for your vision is the promise of what you shall one day be; your ideal is the prophecy of what you shall at last unfold. Bless you, Mary.

HELEN MARSH The ceiling was mosaic with a preponderance of yellow tones, a diamond pattern in yellow and maroon. I felt overwhelmed by colors from the Arc of Spiritual Red, especially the 4th ray – the ray with red, purple, maroon and yellow stripes -

higher forces entering the Path, where one is willing to lay down the "old man," ready for the "new," twice born.

MIRIAM WILLIS   Here in the earth school, we're given the opportunity to develop Christ Consciousness. When we express a willingness to lay aside the "old man"—old habits and faults—that 4th Ray of Spiritual Red gives a powerful message to our subconscious. We become aware of our oneness, spiritual beings within a physical body. New challenges are overcome because of our willingness to change.

MARY What you were seeing is one of the towers of the Temple of Illumination. The towers tie in with the Arc of Yellow.

JEANNE I had a few impressions. I saw trees that looked like Chinese cypress, tall and skinny. Then in a room, a cubicle I was in, I saw a gold bronze cross at right angles. I looked through that to see there was something beyond it. Then I saw a fabric in the color of the purple of faith, white with pink flowers in the middle. It was satiny but more beautiful than satin. When I woke, it was like I had been imprinted, something had been stamped in me or on me. It was different than anything I had ever had before. I kept seeing that, the color kept coming and impressing itself in me.

MARY That's developing power.

ROWENA MEEKS Thursday morning, a few words I received were law, fidelity, respect for love, make room for all of these. Maybe this was a preparation.

MARY That's wonderful. It goes with our pledges.

RALPH   Last night, while we were having our healing meditation, a phrase hit me like a thunderbolt: "and the walls of Jericho shall come tumbling down."

MARY   Yes, because any resistance when we go to the Temple of Illumination, the walls of Jericho really begin to come tumbling down. You see your traits so that you can be illumined about them.

If we can express illumination to the degree that we can heal ourselves.

We ask that through this Temple you will find the creative power and the God-consciousness that are available to you in the Temple of Illumination.

You're beginning to see yourselves as you need to see your egos and your dispositional traits in order to step into illumination, and illumination is not far away. There is not one that does not desire it, and no one is to be denied it. Those were Christ's very words. So if we do become illumined with God's love, we want to express it to the degree that we can heal ourselves, heal ourselves of these lower emotions.

MIRIAM WILLIS Mount to the heights on the stairway of illumination in humility and love. Look deep within and pray always for cleansing. Though you be clean, still penetrate more deeply in humble desire to have the eternal light uncover any stumbling block which may be hidden in the inner self, a bottleneck to progress. Look calmly and with complete confidence, knowing that the penetrating ray cleanses and heals as it reveals. Then leave the growth to the Father.

Ascend, knowing each step on this stairway is a rock of salvation. There are the slow times and the dull times, but remember, his light and love and joy change not. We need varying degrees of discipline on this stairway of life, and it takes a deal of climbing. But let patience have its perfect work that Christ be formed within and shine out in brilliant radiance to bless and guide. This Illumination is the radiation of light. As such it might be called "the fruit of light," or its perfume.

Such radiation is needed, for effective prayer extends outward and inward in actual carrying as potent and real as radio sound waves. See in your mind the power of God as a great vortex reaching down to people who in turn reach up in prayer, adoration and love, the littleness of Earth caught up into the greatness of Heaven as a drop of water is absorbed in the ocean. Real prayer is enveloped in the power of God and transformed with healing grace to the object of its blessing, framed in the investiture of pure spirit to meet the need of that for which the prayer has been offered.

The soul who prays much grows and becomes a ground wire for ever greater radiation of the fused power of God. Therefore, to pray without ceasing brings its own reward and mightily extends the kingdom of Heaven upon the Earth. Would that the hearts of men could realize the tremendous power of fervent prayer. Real prayer sends out rays of luminosity, effective, potent and glorious.

The omniscient word is the all creating expressing. The formless becomes manifested in the formed. By the word of the Lord were the heavens made and the host by the breath of his mouth. Christ is the expression of God, human and divine, perfect and entire, possessing all power; yet he said, I and the Father are one; of my self I can do nothing.

Though he was divine, this perfection was not contained within himself as a separate, independent possession. Rather by virtue of it, he was essentially one with the universal life of the Father. This life flow was constant as the breath he breathed. Just so, it is in varying degrees with all things. No thing has life independent in itself. It is the union of the inward and the outward.

All Nature must breathe to live. And as it is in the natural, so it is in the spiritual. Go searching deep into the heart of life, there to find freedom of spirit in spirit, the righteousness of inspiration, the true soul development, which is divine truth, love, wisdom, and illumination.

JANE We know that our tests on the Other Side are followed by parallel tests in our earth lives. I believe I had one such test on both sides of life. The unexpected earth event was one of the most challenging I've ever experienced.

My nighttime experience began being with others waiting in a large space, hoping to see two different individuals about something of importance in my life. This was a busy area with lots of people milling around. I was on one side of a room; a friend was on the other side. Waiting for what I wanted to happen became overly long and I wandered off to try to speed things up.

In the process, I got lost in the enormous building, kept going into wrong areas and couldn't find my way out of a seeming maze. I asked directions many times, but nobody was of any help. At long last, I finally managed to exit the building, thinking if I could locate the main entrance from the building's exterior, I would be able to get a fresh start and find the area where I needed to go inside.

But once outside, I discovered to my chagrin that the building had no main entrance. I circled around several times to no avail; I was unable to find any way to gain entry again. The building was deserted, located in a derelict area of town with no life around it. The exterior was like a ghost town. I tried to use the building's buzz-in system, which was posted on a wall outside. There was an announcement board like the kind we have outside supermarkets and in laundromats, but this unfortunately contained no printed information, only poorly handwritten items tacked onto purple slips of paper that were very hard to read.

Some way or other, I'm not sure how, I did manage to get inside the building again, where I was able to place a phone call on a pay phone in the lobby. I looked down at the floor and saw that a bag I'd been carrying containing my money, ID, credit cards, everything I needed to function in life, was gone, stolen. I was unsure what to do next, having lost my means of operating in the world, but strangely, I felt no fear or frustration over this loss. Instead, I was confident that despite all obstacles, I would be able to make my way again.

****

THE TEMPLE OF ANIMATION OF GOD'S LOVE

Our prayer on entering the temple: Oh Infinite Alchemist, animate and spiritualize us! Turn our weakness into strength, our wrong thoughts into truth perceptions. Transform our ugly demons of selfishness into blissful wisdom, and our base ores of inertia into purified gold of spiritual development.

We waited expectantly, gazing aloft along the heavens as they stretched away beyond and above us. There they lay like a gigantic carpet of silk unrolled and falling, all flounced and pleated, like a cascade of waters prismatic in the heavenly sunlight. Eventually their dominant colors merged into one, scintillating in celestial radiance like jewels on a kingly crown. Then as we watched, the farthest line within our vision slowly began to change its coloring. We awaited the arrival of our teachers. As they advanced, we began to feel the glow which suffused us with a sense of love and realization of the blessed privilege of our night work.

The temple is set in a vast glade amidst a forest land from which there emerge into the open many roads that branch off into paths in all directions, leading to many spheres where one contacts their own spiritual teachers. One is usually very much aware of a change in one's every day living thereafter. The temple is not circular in shape, but rather oval. At one end of the oval there projects from the forest edge a high broad porch flanked by trees on either side, and above the trees there appears a wing of a building with a balcony running high up the wall and giving a fair view over the glade.

The remaining building is embosomed in the forest, except the towers and dome, which you see soaring above the porch and beyond it. Were it not for these, you wouldn't know there was a large group of buildings there, so thick are the trees about them.

There are five towers, four of equal size, but not patterned alike. In the midst of the four towers of the Temple of the Animation of God's Love, we enter a domed area to climb a great staircase to the most powerful tower. This tower has a mystical significance which only those who have climbed to the holy mount fully understand. The four towers are named: Tower of Sleeping Life, and Tower of Dreaming Life, Tower of Waking Life, Tower of Consciousness.

As we filed out of the temple, music grew in volume, and the atmosphere took on a certain mistiness, becoming transparent and seeming to be flowing both up, down and from within outward like liquid glass of many colors. The Voice said: "Religion is a life and not a ceremony."

After this experience one is completely aware of his failure to understand the use of development. The Voice speaks these words: "Development of God's love made manifest is to be lived. Through this gift, man receives his direction for each day."

Each soul is potentially divine. You as a class were asked to believe and come to realize this channeled teaching is refined until it meets the spiritual needs of the developed soul. Without gladness in one's life, spiritual development comes slowly. Man was created with his goal being to manifest the divine within by controlling his nature, external and internal. By work and worship, he becomes free. Love is the whole of religion. From the desert of your heart, let God's healing waters start.

ESTHER BARNES I have something from the Temple of the Animation of God's Love. A golden cup studded with rubies in the form of a cross is found in the this temple. It rests on an altar in a room with a blue-vaulted dome flooded with golden light. The altar cloth is made of a white silken material with golden tassels.

As we stand before the altar, the golden light fills our being. It is here that we ask for further illumination, and if granted, we drink from the chalice. We then are instructed about means to implement our pledges. God's love animates us. The garden of this temple is filled with blue, white and golden flowers. We see them if we have drunk of the cup.

Then later I got this: blue is the Christ Way; gold from the Temple of Illumination, which was the previous temple we visited, white was purity of motive, the Path of white, the color that contains all colors.

MIRIAM WILLIS Conscious of a great company of men and

angels, we are arrayed in our keynote colors, standing in an area of vastness with an invigorating peach rose glow. Our joy of awareness is keen. One seems to care for all creation more than ever before. One is not conscious of self but only of God's love, which is everywhere and here consciously received. A throng is standing on a spiral in the love center of everything. Soft music like many fountains plays. The great Voice proclaims: "Love is Life, the triumph of the Law. Love one another and ye shall live."

RALPH In meditation, I saw a candle in a ruby red glass with a purple band, the color of faith.

WILLARD I saw a high range of mountains and a drop-off into a valley enveloped in translucent colors.

SYLVIA At first I saw only one small round pool located in a courtyard, which I had come upon after walking on sapphire blue sands. Then I noticed there were more pools all in a semi circle, each having a tone of its own and its own color. The central pool is spacious. It's first pink, then the 11th and 12th rays of spiritual blue. All pools are fed from the central pool. There's a fountain in the center of the pools.

A guide directed me to one of the pools for cleansing and healing in waters of psychological adjustment. One goes to the pool of his particular development. Each ray of the spiritual aura needs cleansing. There are twenty-one archways in the main part of the temple in an almost hidden area in the center.

VIOLET In this temple, I received deeper spiritual power. One is aware of being changed chemically, of spiritual advancement. One feels oriented.

WILLARD In a dream, I went to this land where there were colonnades similar to Corinthian columns. When I got past the columns and went inside the temple, I noticed a group of priests with clerical collars. I was trying to arrange statuary in an altar area, especially three pieces. One was a tall statue, a modernistic thing. I wondered if there was any significance to that.

MARY All right, Margaret, you were in that same Temple with the colonnades. You brought back something similar.

MARGARET Yes, the Temple of the Animation of God's Love.

MARY Willard, you've been given a real picture, so now work on it and see what you can bring out.

JOHN BASINSKI I saw a boat bathed in light that was floating in and out of my line of sight. This was part of a water test in this temple.

HELEN VON GEHR Like Sylvia, I saw a temple in the rays of the Spiritual Arc of Blue. I was very moved by the colors I saw, especially the 11th ray, sky blue, the spiritual ray on which selfless prayers travel, and the 12th ray, the light iridescent sky blue, meaning 4th dimensional consciousness and the realization of man as a spiritual being, which develops a consciousness of the oneness of the visible and invisible worlds. When touching this height, one finds a blessing, a sense of comfort and companionship, a feeling of never being alone.

PATTI I was in a room of blues and sea greens. It was like being beneath water. I knelt at an altar, feeling more deeply and vitally endowed with life. I was acutely aware of taking a water test.

MARY We call it a water test because fear has to be taken out. We're certainly fearful. The water comes up to our chin; our feet aren't touching anything. Many say it's like drowning. All of a sudden, the water seems to envelop you for a moment. In that small moment we're underwater. When we come up, it's like we've never lived before. You know who you are.

JEANNE I had a deep, meaningful experience that ended in a water test. Initially I was in a small room, standing in front of a table behind which was one of our guides on the Other Side. The teacher left after a short conversation and I wanted to find him again. He had told me where I could reach him so I went to that location. Two large events were taking place there. At the first event, a big crowd was waiting to get into a central auditorium. I went past this group to another room, where another big crowd was sitting at tables, eating in the dark. Since I was unable to locate the teacher at either venue, I went to the information desk but could find no information I was seeking there, either.

A woman friend and I decided to leave together. We started out on a lawn that led to pavement and a busy road. Some annoying people were nipping at our heels, so my friend went to the other side of the street to get away from them. Suddenly it wasn't a street anymore but an enormous body of water. I had to dodge waterway interferences at first, but then that subsided and now, alone, I was doing the breast stroke, then the crawl in a vast, very deep but calm body of water.

I felt alone yet not isolated. The distance I was to swim looked formidable, almost endless. The body of water was reminiscent of the Great Lakes – Lake Michigan, Lake Ontario. I kept swimming. The water was so pure, pristine and refreshing. Ahead, I could make out the shore, but it was so far, far away that I understood it would take a long time, strength and endurance to swim all that distance to the opposite side. The water also reminded me of Lake Constance, the lake that borders Germany, Austria, and Switzerland, where if you looked for the shore, it would be very far away or even invisible, like the distant shores of another world. I had a feeling of endlessness, yet confidence that all was well, and that I was on the right path.

******

THE TEMPLE OF ADORATION

A sub-temple in the Temple of Animation of God's Love

MARGARET This is the Temple of Adoration. At first one has the impression of soft pink corals of a very light shade, all pulsating. They form many tall, slender arches which go up and out of sight. And tonight during the meditation I saw similar arches which seemed to grow, recede, pulsate and do all sorts of interesting things. Another room has pillars. it has a ceiling. A border around the edge of the ceiling sparkles with pale greens and the daintiest of yellow pinks. These colors glow and ray outward. And then the colors become rosier.

There is a pool here, the wellspring of divine love. The substance looks especially luscious, of a rich apricot hue. A thin circle of deep rose color starts from the center of the pool and travels in a widening circle to the rim, where it disappears. The pool is formed from a deep crystal. It reaches around, beneath and through the bases of the pillars that encircle it. It is labyrinthine. The waters are a deep ice blue.

Bathing in this pool, one is healed of misconceptions. The pool is fed from below as well as above by selfless outpourings adoring the nature of God, coming from both higher and lower planes. Human love, when it reaches this high a state, is pure, radiant, glowing.

A dip in the pool leaves one near joyful tears because of the beauty of it and the gratitude for being allowed to come. One learns here that permeability is not something one has or doesn't have. Each new color quality needs practice before one can hold it. Like water on an oily surface, a new color makes no impression until the oil on the surface of the old mode is eroded and then dissolved. One must practice the new color so that the old one will be completely removed, and then the new color won't fade out.

The refreshing pool is not shallow. Even all the columns are filled with apricot light; these columns store light. On emerging, one feels rested, loved, loving, and exalted in happy love of God.

I am given the feel of the vibrations. I had an impression of all peaches, and of pulsating apricots lighter than ordinary apricot. Several arches form from a source I can't see. They reach outward toward me. In another room with pillars, there is a border around the ceiling in pale greens, yellow and pinks, all in light and in colors that sparkle, glow and ray out as they become rosier.

MARY   That is preparation for the Eightfold Path in the Corridor of Adoration.

ESTHER BARNES I was in another meditation room; there are seven different rooms around this Corridor.

PATTI I saw blackbirds sitting on a wire. This gave me quite a reaction. I felt upset about it.

MARY   Those blackbirds signify worries, especially because they're sitting on the wire; therefore they have settled themselves. The message to Patti is: stop worrying. Release the old so that new concepts may be fulfilled.

MIRIAM WILLIS   We're tested many times in seeing unpleasant things. Our nervous system reacts very quickly if we're offended.

KATIE BASINSKI I dreamed of a baby with a bandaged leg and that had me worried, too. What could that signify?

MARY Something rather irksome is coming. The bandage is the waiting.

CARMEN AUSTIN Outside the Temple in the quiet of soundless semi-twilight, I saw shadows of butterflies and a muted gold light. Mist comes through the golden light and lifts.

MARY We can declare the glow of a sunrise and a sunset. That's God's love. Think of all we're given. In this temple, we all feel so grateful that this has been our opportunity. In our prayer of thanks, we say: "Oh God, we have so much." Seek always to live under the glow of the result of your night work.

It's the greatness within us that allows us to enter these temples. It's important that there must be a true yearning and desire, or you couldn't be taken here.

****

THE TEMPLE OF EXTENSION OF DEVELOPMENT

I ask you to accept this statement, "Out of the silence will come the vision and the voice." Silence, like perfection, is a wholeness which cannot be diminished or disturbed by any elimination or addition. Accordingly, man will come into his own as heir apparent to life eternal through visions of immortality and the knowledge of guidance given through instruction in the temples of the Heaven World.

Like attracts like, the deep sounds unto the deep, but only in a golden moment of God's grace do the two, the soul and the oversoul, embrace each other in completeness. However, when this golden moment shall arrive, no one can predict.

Great joy accompanies illumination. From this Temple of the Extension of Consciousness, through spiritual development the seeker declares, "What I have seen is unsurpassable. All that you see and feel is God's unending revelation, manifestation of the hidden holy, where the marriage of human and divine rests on an all-inclusive accord and identity."

When the Voice speaks out of the heart of the silence of the boundless, one has been blessed with a vision of the future which holds the map, meter, and mettle of their life. A miracle has shown them the Path Eightfold, happiness in balanced living, the scales of Life.

MIRIAM WILLIS It has always helped me to realize the logic of the continuity with which God seems to deal with us as we climb and grow. It's like an unbroken pillar of light within that becomes more brilliant and reflects its brilliance more often through our soul and our memory to our conscious mind.

And then, through this process and the pattern of prayer referred to, we find that the earthly power within the temple of our being and the heavenly that seems to reach down to us and infill us through our night training become more unified, like the glowing peach color of the union of mind and spirit in the Channel of our Being. And we find that our prayer reaches farther.

What is this but an expansion of spiritual growth? You have had flashes as you've prayed for people when you suddenly see them, you sense them or you feel them. You pray for them and the law of attraction or the vibration on which you ride, or your colors that flow to that person change because of the direction to the person. And you feel the difference, don't you?

Isn't this an extension, an expansion of the spirit within us? So perhaps each one of us can realize this with a greater poignancy and continuity of growth than we have before, if we just expect that memory within us to be quickened and the outreach of the suspension and the extension, the expansion of consciousness to increase.

GENE I had a dream that I think is appropriate. I was driving my car. I understand the car represents your body. The road was familiar to me, but all of a sudden I came to a part where it was changed, and I found myself on the wrong side of the road. In order to get back on the right side, I turned sharply to the right and went into a service station. And then, all of a sudden my car disappeared.

MARY You must have changed vehicles, didn't you? Maybe you're not just "riding along" with it on the substance of your mentality, and it could be that in the changing of vehicles the Teachers expressed it that way to you. You see, one of the things that they do in order to train us, is to take something we're very familiar with and start us out on our old track. Then they show us we're either saved from a mistake, or we're stopped in our tracks, wandering around helplessly without knowing how we're going to find our way back. I think you've all had that experience. "What am I here for? I never was here before."

Then something familiar comes up, and from there you seem to find your way. Many times you're with people; and sometimes you're without, just stumbling along. But eventually you come out in the open realization: "This is some kind of a test I'm being given." Probably there was a powerful thought sent to you that you should change your ways.

GENE I thought it meant, ok, so you don't need the physical body. Eventually you won't have it anymore, and you'll still be alive.

MARY I wouldn't have put that construction on it, but it's very good. On thinking it through, I think, in truth, you have changed your road, have you not?

GENE I think so.

MARY Yes. Because you have quite steadily for quite some time thought along the same lines, watching for improvement, every day traveling the road of life. I'm seeing the hardship and the easy going, but if you have to turn around and hunt for a road and if it isn't as pleasant when you enter it, many times you take a detour right then. And there is then a lapse of time when you seem to do nothing.

JEANNE   Mary, would that state be what you've called the "wasteland of the soul?"

MARY   We go along in our development a long time, and it doesn't seem to amount to anything; we're at what I would call the wasteland or the desert, where there's nothing that seems to move a person from where they are. Yes, they have development just so far, but what's the use of going on?

One person said to me, "I see less of the colors than I did a year ago." I asked, "Are you developing otherwise? " "No. I don't think so." I said, "Why don't you stop for a while? Do something else." In a couple of weeks they were back. They'd had time to think it over. They began to keep track of little things that had happened. We do have what we call "the touch system," that reaches out into this desert of our souls, and every once in a while there's a thought or a touch of the divine. We've met up with a higher force, and the soul is urging us to come back into the light of understanding ... because the soul wants expression. The ears want to hear; the eye wants to see.

If a person wishes to evolve, they use the three bodies, physical, mental and spiritual. To carry with us as a pack on our back the spiritual body unused —we would never meet our spiritual body if we couldn't go into a higher state of imagination that touches the emotional body that causes us to take the chance of something that might seem farfetched to another person.

When we've had these little touches of spiritual awakening, and we feel that the aura has developed to the place where it incorporates within itself a welcoming vibration, and when this thing is there before us for a moment as the sight of something very beautiful, or the opening of a door into the spiritual world for just a moment, and we have seen it, it isn't a thing that you go out on the street and tell, but rather, it's a treasure you hold quietly to yourself.

Thoughts are living things. And when you're contradicting something that's not understood, you've soiled that something. So then once again, I call that the wasteland of the soul, where things are wasted. You have a gift and you haven 't used it. And if that does happen to you, place it in your treasure box and keep the lid down, because you'll be using it so often.

These are usable – not imaginary things, but usable traits that cause man to become one with humanity. It causes the kingdom of the soul to operate out to where the fullness of God's love extends to where it's needed. It travels on Color; it travels on sound; it moves and has its being in the higher realms of understanding. Wisdom carries the golden color that all knowledge is held within. Worship has incorporated a certain amount of wisdom, or it would not have lasted.

So there are times when life doesn't seem to be pushing you; we go into the desert of our being. Eventually life becomes less irksome and we find the desert of our life in bloom. Before that, we were wondering, hunting for the River of Life and flowers to bless us. One of the reasons we often miss taking the right road or doing the right thing is that as we look at it, we decide, why change? There's a responsibility facing me if I make a change. If I make that change, I won't be posited in the same way, and it's annoying to be in new surroundings and feel goaded into doing something at just that time.

We all want freedom of action and freedom of thought. The greatest freedom comes when you get into that world where action isn't evident but the ongoing of the soul itself seems to be the guide. And we're never bored with life. We're truly busy. We don't find time for the things we used to do and we wonder why. Because we're under soul direction. Our day goes so swiftly, whereas it used to be just the opposite. We're seriously thinking not only of our life, but often about the lives of other people who affect us. Therefore, you're embracing the irksome things of the path as well as the bright and joyful.

RALPH I wonder if I was driving on the same road that Gene was. I was on a road pock-marked by shell fire, roughest road I've ever seen in my life.

MARY Around New Year's, we were on a very unusual mission, and you saw some of the things we don't care to see. We saw bombs dropping. You weren't close enough to see the bombs hit people, but we did see great explosions, we saw things going up in the air. And we came back with a powerful desire to at least bend every effort of our consciousness toward the cessation of war. Let's keep that in mind and thank God for the freedom we have had in the past, and then let us look forward to it again.

JEANNE   What Gene said reminded me that I saw a change also this week. I was standing at right, watching. On the left was my horse, who was going to be clipped. And then all of a sudden, my horse turned into a girl, and they were cutting her hair.

MARY Well then, there must be something being created in the universal way of a gentleness in you or in some interest that you're having. Maybe, in reaching out, the next thing you write may show that very plainly that you're going to bring a gentility in. And that's also applying it to your everyday life. Besides that, you may have felt that even that animal, the horse you ride, can be induced to being more gentle. These are some applications to the things that come to us. Dreams are living things, if we're trying for the Path.

******

THE TEMPLE OF WATERS OF LIFE

Jesus – the perfect example of the Waters of Life. The earliest written and probably the most authentic account of the illumination of Jesus runs as follows: "And straightway coming up out of the water, he saw the Heavens rent asunder, and the spirit of a dove descending upon him, and a voice came out of the heavens saying, 'This is my beloved son, in whom I am well pleased."

To all who experience going to this temple, for a short time after coming up out of the waters, a veil is lifted from the eyes of the mind, permitting the sight clearness of space; and the standard of life is distinctly different when the seeker realizes he must find solitude of soul, as he has been renewed to go forth in faith and find his place in the Kingdom.

The seeker senses his baptism and feels his soul cry for release. He has experienced visions sublime, indescribable divine intoxication when the cloud of silence burst and its merciful drops rained upon him. He knew that when the river of spirit overran the boundaries of his soul, baptizing him in the waters of eternity, that the drought of ignorance was banished by the shower of blessings: the petals of the flower of past-present-future opened and revealed to him the intricate beauty of God's plan for each soul.

MIRIAM WILLIS   We find ourselves in a circular garden surrounding this great temple of translucent loveliness. The gardens are like the spokes of a wheel, the temple itself being the hub, with each section being a different species of flora that indicates areas of development. The paths are smooth still waterways reflecting many colors, as ineffable light plays upon them. Everything has a glow of exquisite freshness, like a kiss of the morning dew. Delicate fragrance fills the air.

One walks or glides along river paths, pausing in stillness whenever prompted from within to meditate. The channel of concentration between one's inner self and the colorful beauty of the flowers reveal to one's understanding qualities they symbolize, disclosing the happy knowledge of endowment already developed.

Each section leads to an entrance of veiled light. Passing through, we are enveloped in a blinding light, clothed in white. As our vision clears through this brilliance, we are drawn to a large pool of water. The attraction is irresistible; we walk steadily forward as the water deepens about us, until all but our head, held high, is immersed. We have gone to a great depth. It's hard to breathe, as fear all but overtakes us. However, the waters gradually become shallower and we step forth on the farther side not the least bit wet, clothed in our keynote color.

We are conscious of our Sponsor as we receive the blessing of "well done." For this, a culmination of many water tests, is the deepest, highest cleansing we have yet received. It is part of the initiation to the Eightfold Path in the Temple of the Waters of Life.

LENORE I was aware of going through gradations of loveliness. Everything was clear as crystal, in an all enveloping kind of beautiful suspension. A great central light gleamed with glory as companies of angels appeared. Deep silence permeated, yet the stillness was full with joy. Trumpets and other instruments began playing as the great light took a form like unto the Christ. Conscious of praise, thanksgiving and adoration, I was given the communion cup. I promised to minister especially to babies and to the dying.

MARY I believe that we can walk in eternity now. We can be just as well with the other side as we can be here. We can know it's one world without end. Say it to yourself and see what comes out of it. It's like a mantra when repeated. It becomes something that the

Lord said at the end of his prayer: "One world without end, amen." It's a glorious thought, the ongoing of the human soul. If this life be a day in school, it has taken a lot of training.

Now things pass; they leave their scars, and our thinking must change if the scars are to heal. We can certainly keep the scars from healing in our consciousness if we go over and over again the hardship of living with them.

MIRIAM WILLIS   The Temple of the Waters of Life seems to reach into infinitude. Its transparent walls are like unto running waters, shading from deep marine blue and greens to lighter tones of sparkling light, touched with all delicate colors merging into mother-of-pearl.

LOLA As each prayer is dropped as a pebble into the deep pool of the Waters of Life, ripple after ripple created flows out from the central source in ever-widening bands. The first ripple becomes very large in circumference, flowing to the very edge of the pool; their vibrations carry it into the surrounding area, continuing in an ever widening, all inclusive circle of blessing. Prayer took you to the center of the pool to the top of the temple on which you stood to observe the ripples, the outreach of your prayers.

Now you start your descent into the Waters of Life. It is as if you are on an elevator that stops at different levels, indicated by the color of the water. At each level, some step out into the water, and others step into the elevator.

Each one's needs are known; each one's keynote color illumines our whole being. Having been bathed in the essence of life at each needed level, we gather together in a huge central chamber. As we enter the waters of this chamber, we feel an even greater exhilaration than the cleansing experience on our previous levels.

We walked in a floating movement without effort, as rippled bands of color moved from the beautiful 8th of blue, modifying to the 9th of blue - truth of self attained – to the 10th, reality of message, to the 11th, spiritual life. We kneel in selfless prayer for those who have guided us along life's path, for the great teachers who have brought us God's truth and helped keep us balanced that we might stay on the path.

Our co-mingled colors send forth rays of nourishment to the people of the world, a prayer for peace that was generated in this great community gathering on waves of gratitude.

We then entered the center, the wellspring, azure iridescent blue, and our awareness into 4th dimensional consciousness was expanded, as sparkling drops of this color literally washed away the outer. We stood renewed in the presence and received the cup of life which we gratefully drank as a benediction.

MARGARET One of the ways of entering this temple is by water. I saw a canoe-like boat with a single seat so smooth on the inside it reminded me of a ceremonial temple boat. The outside was carved, the boat was pointed at both ends. The water was a deep, deep blue. I got in and noticed that overhead and to the side was rough hewn stone, a natural cave. There, a shimmering light straight ahead led the way. There are no oars or paddles; the boat just glides on its own. I go into a tunnel, an extremely large, brilliantly lighted arena. The light is so bright I can't see.

BARBARA I'm standing on a portico facing a row of Gothic arches. The sky appears to be light, with blush orchid, my keynote color, the color of serenity, showing through the archways. I step through one of the archways and walk down steps to a blue pool of crystal water. As I become immersed, all earth's ills drop away. A voice speaks, saying: you are healed. I now see that the arches encircle the pool, and as I look up from the pool to the side opposite the one I entered, I see the sky brighten beyond the arches in colors of salmon pink, peach, pale yellow, opalescent greens and blues, cascading down until they are reflected in the pool and seem to become a part of me.

MIRIAM ALBPLANALP   The words that came to me upon awakening were that this ceremony we experienced seemed like a real baptism.

SYLVIA As I peer into the depths of a small round pool, I feel that to let myself be absorbed to its depths would cleanse me of any clinging errors of my past. So with hardly a ripple, my body slipped into it silently as a knife into a sheath. Its stark depths swallowed me and I was absorbed into a well of peaceful darkness.

Walking into the courtyard of the temple upon sapphire blue granules of sand, my bare feet sought the comfort of an individual pool that lined the walls.

Listening to the music of the great geyser or fountain in the center of this circle of pools, one hears each pool echoing a different note of the falling droplets of the fountain ringing with a tone and brilliance of its corresponding color as it sounds.

A solid brilliant color for a moment, its note sounded, then returned to the natural reflecting tone of water. I was entranced with this joyous panorama of sound and color, and would have bodily entered the fountain, but each step I meant to take toward it seemed to propel me farther away from it. Later I learned that the fountain was the perfect symphony of all the colors and music, and in my imperfect state, I would have found entrance into its exciting vibration painful. Instead, a hooded guide touched me lightly on the shoulder, and I turned and followed her into a the depths of a small court far to the right, and here dropped silently into the first pool for my healing.

I felt like a small cell in the bloodstream of a great being. As these waters of psychological adjustment penetrated my memory patterns, cleansing and healing them, I felt as one in a dream during illness, direct from wakefulness into a nightmarish panorama of past fears and dreams. I could feel the heaviness of the past gently loosen from my mind, and a heady refreshment of clear liquid light entering, replacing the mud of illusion.

I think I sang. At least music came through me. As I felt the rushing waters enter and re-enter the channels of my thought, finding parched areas of consciousness that soaked in the water as rain on the desert, my being transformed from arid waterless waste into flower gardens of nectar and honey. This was just the first pool of a great semicircle of them that lined the outer wall of the courtyard, each partially enclosed.

The paths and hallways connected them so that one might proceed to the pool that his development responded to. I have entered other pools since that night, for each new ray of one's spiritual aura requires this process of renewing to withstand the challenge of Earth's tests. Never have I been so deeply moved.

Each time we go, we enter through an outer wall edged at top with a darker tile that sweeps up in reverse scallops so that each arched entrance in the wall is peaked above. The wall sweeps around in a great circular front with twenty-one archways for entering.

We always entered the same door and waited in a group to be beckoned into the active part of the temple. There is a hidden area in the center which I have never entered. Such things of Earth of which I have not wished to be healed remain under cover. The very center of the temple which contains a slightly larger pool than the others, I yet have to partake of. This pool is opalescent blue and then pink.

All the pools are fed from this central pool which gushes high as a fountain which I first mentioned. I suspect all the pools are also fountains that shoot upward toward the center and merge in the central fountain.

VIOLET   One receives in this temple a deeper penetration of spiritual power because of the revelation and realization of the constant flowing and feeding of that power to the soul of man. One is changed chemically in spiritual advancement. The phrase "the wellspring from on high" that has visited us now has meaning, and one can say with understanding: give us this day our daily bread. The light of understanding has cleared the mind of uncertainties, and one's goal in life has become vivid. One is orientated and ready to return to the living of life with a freshness of outlook and a purer perception.

MIRIAM ALBPLANALP   I must have awakened with a query whether we made any extra vows, because the message I received starts out: "You made no additional vows last night. These had been made prior to your privilege of going to receive the energy increases to put in action. You received a chemical booster last night." My question: would there be a sort of kerosene to make the flame burn brighter? The answer: The degree and quantity of love energy is boundless; the limiting factor is your ability to receive, transmute and then express it.

The class last night was aided in stretching our grasp of another's need, for the human heart is such that when a need is recognized, it sets up an equal desire to fill that need. The same principle exists as physical law as anything rushing in to fill a vacuum to keep all in balance. Earth channels have become clogged and closed, therefore unbalanced conditions result and there is a constant struggle for balance.

God's higher laws parallel laws now known. Some laws are not understood accurately, but the principle of parallelism is our point. Sufficient for now.

MARY   That was part of last night. Keep track of it.

ESTHER BARNES   I remember a courtyard, a huge fountain, and lots of people.

GRACE   It's the first time this has ever happened to me. I'm so happy about it. I stood on a landing, looked down on four or five marble stairs that were curved on the end.

MARY   That's good. Now you climb those stairs.

JOHN   The reading of these things apparently brought this back to mind. All I remember is something like a boat, but it wasn't in water so much as it seemed to be so light that it was almost like a gas. It didn't fill the room, but it was like being in the Blue Grotto of Capri, lighter, yet you're in it, floating in and floating out. The boat wasn't on top of it; this water seemed to fill it, yet the boat wasn't sinking. Then it seemed like I was floating in this, being part of it. I remembered that I've had this experience before.

MARY   Yes, you've had many water tests before.

HELEN VON GEHR   Yesterday morning, I had the impression of powerful reflections. There was a great forecourt. The temple itself was of the 11th or 12th of blue - very soft, pastel blues. In the forecourt were five reflector discs, flat, together in a unit of five, but I got the impression that there might be more, perhaps twelve of these disks. In each one that I saw in front of me was a reflection of things in the Heaven world, of things to come that we would see in time.

During meditation, I was concentrating on this to see if there was anything else I could bring back. I saw a teacher in the most shimmering beautiful white robe. She took me over to the discs, and said it's not time yet to see what is being reflected in these; you have to be ready for these things. Of course, this applies to all of us, not to me personally.

PATTI   It seems like such a marvelous experience, it's hard to call it a test. Most of the water tests I've been through have been pretty rugged experiences. I realize water tests are to clear fear. Miriam mentioned in hers that this was a culmination.

MARY   We have to trade our fears for faith. If we really have faith, if we really want to go the whole way, then fear has to be taken out. That's the reason we call it a test. Because when you go down into this bowl for immersion, you are certainly fearful. The water comes over you; you are to the depths, your feet are not on the bottom of anything. I believe dozens of people have said to me after they have come out, it was like drowning, you didn't know whether or not you were going down for the last time. There is our fear we had taken with us. Then all of a sudden the water seems to envelop you for just a moment, and in that small moment of being under that water, our spiritual immersion results in something miraculous happening to us.

We have to have the faith to go down into the water. You come up as if you had never lived before. The life forces within you, the spirit is awakened to expression, and you know who you are.

The largest thing I have ever seen is the mercy of our Father in giving us the privilege of entering the living waters. That is eternity. That is living in eternity now, that is living into larger life, entering the larger life we have read about that has been spelled in words and form to us. We have to somehow let it enter the interior of our bodies. Cleansing the interior of man, a really true housecleaning once in awhile, is the most wonderful thing we can have.

You don't go back often. It's a privilege to be asked back. This is something that's given you as a chance. God gives it to you, the chance to take this Eightfold Path, the path of living the life. It means seeing the other person before you see yourself. It means stepping in the shade so that the other person can walk in the sun, remembering at all times that I and the Father are one, the self respect that one has to develop in order to live that life.

We have none of us on earth so far become christed, as our great Christ was, master of all. But his teaching is so simple that a child can be taught. The depths of it are so great that we are up to our throats in its depths. If we got to thinking about it, if once in awhile we can go back and be washed clean of all of these envies, these unclean thoughts, the everlasting living each day as if it could not be endured— many people live that day. They live to the day of rest, to the end of the week. And who can blame them? But every day can be a Sabbath, every day a happy day. The Sabbath was supposed to be a very happy day in the history of the Jewish people. As I look back on every Sabbath of my life that I can remember, there was always something special.

If we once start on this path of development, we richly deserve to go to the Temple of the Waters of Life. And there are many other temples that have such revelation that you have no concept of now. Neither did you when we took the Temple of Creation when we first started out. You had no idea there was this special temple. Did you notice in the temples you've had, there have been no two alike? They're all temples, yes, but they all have the intrinsic value that we've needed in our daily lives for living with each other.

I do say this: until man himself finds peace in his own heart, he can't expect his brother to be at peace or to tell his brother how to live. So it's peace within ourselves, the finding of the law. Our dear ones have gone over and we have asked, what is it like? Where are they? The simple quest of trying to find out... you have a right to know. I can take the Good Book and over and over again and there's nothing hidden. Seek and ye shall find, knock and it shall be opened to you. I can stay right in the New Testament and give you every evidence that you have a right to know about the heaven world, and that's what Christ came to the world for.

CLARA JACKSON When I first started meditation, I was aware of a gold pitcher pouring sparkling water into a gold ball within my cupped hands. Later, I became aware of walking through a pale rose light. I then found myself on a rounded path with green slopes on either side. On the right I see a golden light like grades of topaz going up to the sky. As I climb the path, which is steeper than my first impression, I see white wooly sheep grazing on the right side in the distance. I walk a little off the path to just enjoy the beauty of the meadow and the attunement I feel with all things.

Down a hill and a little to the right is a large building that is shining white with big round white columns. In front of this building I see a brook running and cascading downhill, sparkling clear and bubbling with a song. The foliage around the brook is not dense and the are trees well spaced. Overhead is a brilliant blue sky. I am walking along the side of the brook as I follow it down the hill until the brook breaks out of the foliage into clear perfection.

As I breathe in the atmosphere, I become aware of surrounding buildings in pure white with kind of amber shadows. I seem to be in a type of courtyard with the pool being the arched center of interest. I am now going through a large arch-like doorway with gold trim. It's dark inside, but soon I see the dome-shaped walls are the light through blue of reflected water. From the entrance, there are steps that seem to encircle the room and go down to the water. I go into the water, feeling radiant and pure. It is as if I turned from a shadow just seeing what was going on around me to a glowing person that I could see doing things, as well as feel what was going on inside of the person. This person looked altogether different than I looked, but it was me.

I next walked through a rounded hall, each step taking me higher out of the water. I am completely dry. I am wearing a flowing white robe with gold braid around the neck and down the front. I stepped into a dome shaped ornamentation room much larger than the first room I was in. This one is brilliant with light. I am greeted warmly by our group as I enter, although there are no words. I am taken through the crowd - a lot of people are there - to an area on the other side of the room. Here some sit and some stand, as if waiting, but a little apart from the others. The people in our group also did not look the same, but I can recognize those I am closest to by the feeling I have about them.

The next room is just around the corner. This room is colored in the rich hues found deep beneath the surface of the sea. It is as if we were beneath the water and the light is dimmed upon traveling through tons of water.

In the front and to the left as I enter is an area that is lighter, which is like an altar. I go to this altar and kneel before it. As I do, I feel a great warm deep feeling come into me as if I become more deeply and vitally aware of life, my purpose for being, and re-dedicated to my life work.

MARY Thank you Clara. My, we are proud.

KATIE When I got back Wednesday morning, standing on the right was a temple with turrets; I remember white mist or clouds came in front and the bottom part was completely covered before the end of the viewing.

MARY You were getting ready for the Temple of Waters of Life last night. Wednesday night we were given quite a talk on the upcoming temple.

EMILY I had quite a lesson on rhythm, emotion and feeling all bound together one night. I was given a piano lesson, and then took a walk in the hills with a very young person who probably was a teacher. In that walk, we viewed the clouds in the sky of lavender and many shades of light purple – very beautiful.

MARY I would take that, Emily, as a point of faith, and the faith has to be created through great patience. You are starting towards this faith.

ANDREW High on a plateau, surrounded by a grove of trees, the temple takes on the path of higher development. It shows one their soul's path that is before them and how they may tread it. It gives one a picture of their development and the purpose of it. The longer view is shown them, the why to this point and the how of the future. We are taken to a place of mirrors to see this, and then advised by wise ones if one cares for advice. Nothing is forced, it is only shown in a very gentle way. The picture of one's life, past and future possibilities can be brought through if one wants to know strongly enough. This is the key, your own desire and determination of your own efforts and will.

MIRIAM ALBPLANALP Why were so many people involved last night? Was this a special night?

MARY Yes, it's a special night for the Waters of Life. People go for cleansing. It is a very great time, a very great occasion. I have so prayed and longed that your eyes would be opened at such a time, and you would have the faith to say "I saw it."

JOHN I did have a seeing but it had nothing to do with water.

MARY That's all right, there are plenty places around the temple.

JOHN I was carving out a form which seemed to be myself.

MARY   There's one phase of that temple where people place the desires of themselves in a carving. You go the whole long side of that temple, and there is face after face. A person can go and find their own carving. It has gone down through the ages, when man had a flint, and he put his mark on a tree. That's one of the oldest things you can find in history. A boy gets a knife and carves his initial on a tree.

JOHN   But the form was myself and I was molding it in places where I though it should be molded.

MARY   Someone told me they felt a regular mask go over them, that they felt the weight of it and they walked with it. They had to go for help to get it off. When it was taken off, they never dreamed they could look that good. Then they said they walked back, and there it was, that mask in bas relief on the side of the temple. They said, I've been a new person ever since.

HELEN MARSH   I had an experience similar to John's, in that I too saw carvings. I crossed a bridge in hopeful expectation. At right, I saw a building with stone pillars laid out on an expanse of lawn with birch trees. Inside, I faced a delicately, intricately carved wall, the same thing that John mentioned seeing. I then went through a long corridor in all shades of blue to a series of pools, where in one, I experienced a water test in which I thought I was dying. I came out feeling refreshed, renewed, reborn.

MIRIAM ALBPLANALP   Via meditation with regard to the Tesla coil, this is a means of transforming current and its application. It's my impression that we are all transmitters of currents and energies which often need transforming to meet the needs of a situation.

CLARA   Is there a temple that is blue, shimmery like an old fashioned fairytale castle, with a long pathway leading up to it? It goes on both sides and it's kind of hard to get up. I have more on this. I don't have much on the inside. I must have gotten two different pictures.

MARY   Your picture is the temple we're coming to next, the Temple of Incarnation. Did you see steps?

CLARA Yes.

MARY Will you count those steps for me? I know it will be given to you. We go there next Thursday night.

VIOLET   I'd like to ask a question. After the Temples of Incarnations and the Temple of Inception, on our charts it says, "Preparing to meet the Hierarchy." Does that mean that a person being developed at the end of the 7th Plane goes before the Hierarchy for the first time? Had they not been before?

MARY Yes, they have been before. We go before the Hierarchy at the end of every plane.

LOLA You said last week we should try to get something on the Eightfold Path, and then you said you would tell us more about it.

MARY It's a big subject. We're not going to be to the 8th Plane for some time; you have quite a ways to go, but I would like you to approach it with some knowledge, and would like to bring the knowledge of the plane to you that you could incorporate it into your thinking. Then when we get to this Eightfold Path you'll have some consciousness of what you have to accomplish. You're going to meet up with all sorts of "lions along the way." If you can overcome the lions in your disposition, the Eightfold Path will open up to you and you will certainly have experiences.

WILLARD I got that there's a sub temple connected to the Temple of the Waters of Life by way of a labyrinth underground, and there seems to be a tunnel and a pool where the waters are the color of deep ice blue.

LOLA I saw two angels facing each other, the moon gate between them. I was looking out to the ocean. I remember experiencing the water test with the rest of the class.

MARY Father, we ask thy blessing. We in gratitude bow our heads. For the next seven days until we meet again, dear Father, be our guide and our protector. For this and all days of our lives, we thank thee. We ask for peace in the world, and that we ourselves may become peace. Amen.

****

THE TEMPLE OF INCARNATION CHRIST WAY

At this temple, my guardian angel led me through one of the entrances, and I found myself in a spacious chamber filled with subdued light in which various shades of color were blended in such perfect harmony that it struck me as some beautiful and soothing music made visible. The walls here were hung with cloud-like draperies in which greens, pinks, crimson and golds were blended so artistically that nowhere was there a jarring note of color. The draperies were unlike any of earth's textiles. They were distinctly visible to me, but they offered no resistance to my touch. It was like thrusting my hand into a cloud. In the chamber there were several couches whose colors displayed the same harmonious coloring. Many beautiful plants and flowers adorned the area.

I was soon aware of a great volume of blended voices singing in the heavenly garden, and as I was led into the garden, I saw great tiers of choir angels whose beauty of face and form brought joy to my soul.

One master teacher explained death as the unending life, and another spoke on the higher planes that we could attain by living in Christ's teaching and expressing spiritual qualities.

This temple's sublime beauty impressed me deeply. Its marble whiteness covers a great area. It has glorious music, wondrous fragrance, the brilliance of the faces of the angels who abide there. At last it dawned on me: in my previous visits here, it had always seemed like a fine day in June, with so much to see outside and inside -- the broad thoroughfare that seemed lost in the distance, the twenty-one steps at the entrance, the inscribing over the door: "In my Father's house are many mansions."

In our lecture we were told by the great Voice, "To all who earnestly seek to know God and who open their hearts to him, God sends his holy angels to give them spiritual guidance that they may realize they are truly God's children, precious in his sight." These hosts of angels are eager, yearning to minister to mankind, to persuade men to open the windows of their souls to God's light, which brings with it that peace that passeth all understanding.

VIOLET   This temple is crystalline pure in glimmering white. Seven sturdy pillars along the front support the roof. We approached the temple's twenty-one steps. The first step up is narrow; the last step is almost as broad as the whole temple. A strong light is focused on these steps. We walked up a lighted way to enter through illumination. Gradually our eyes adjusted. The music had a gorgeous flute like quality.

MARY   Every human being who goes to this temple keeps an imprint of it that the soul will always remember. If you're one of the people who will do this work out in the world, your path will be given you. Your guardian angel will always be there. We've had planes, temples where we had a particular realization of Christ; this is certainly one of them.

The memory of this temple is one of the most beautiful. This is a place where you know Christ talks. The story of development is so close to Christ's love. That love has to be great, it has to be fulfilled within yourself, running over before you have anything to give. Christ extends His hands over the boundaries, and we know it is one world without end, amen. We sing that right along. This is the example of what Christ meant when he said, I am with you always, even to the end of the world. Where I am, there shall ye be also. That is our first real proof, as we know the everlasting arms that are supporting us there in this particular temple.

Each time you hear the lecture there, they speak of the Christ and the bands he left here and those who are there toiling in the field. To them, it's saving the lives and souls of creatures here on Earth as nearly as they can, perpetuating the work.

Whatever your burden, carry it lightly, for Christ carries half of it. Wash clean you mind of resentment. Whatever you're trying to do of value, first clean house. Go into the house of your mind and clean it of the slippery eels. After you've cleaned it, fill it with beauty. Once we become relaxed, we can enter that spiritual vibration and know we're ready to go. With that, what can we not do?

The Master's voice speaks in these temples. We know the reverberating tones of that voice. The sympathetic understanding is so great that you feel as if you've been given a blessing. We go as a company, and we sit enveloped in the quiet and wait. Eventually, a light develops our aura, and he speaks.

MIRIAM WILLIS   We have heard his words: "In my Father's house are many mansions; if it were not so, I would have told you; for I go to prepare a place for you. I will come again and receive you unto myself, that where I am, there you may be also."

MARY There is within man that which is eternal enlightenment, for which he reaches within. He has nothing he can hold to outside, so he goes within, and within is the kingdom.

MIRIAM WILLIS During the 40 days of Lent, as we now are, universal love is renewed in our hearts.

MARY Lent is very important. The glorification of Christ's life is given us many, many times in this temple. We affirm our love for him. We search ourselves and we are searched. We are walking somewhere. The teachers would like to have us go the entire breadth of the area of the temple before we forget, in order that the temple should stay with us.

Lent shouldn't be a time of grief. It should be a time of partaking of what is offered. And if you really knew the story of Lent as given in the Invisible World, it is for man to take stock of himself and his past year. And through the vision of Lent, the Lenten season is a season of resting and of getting back into the rhythm of the soul.

A chalice within us is taken out at Lenten time. And if that can be, then all the sorrow that goes along with Lent is wiped away, and we have a joyous Lenten time. Think of that when the season comes. It also is a time that one gives up some one thing. If I should ask you to give up one thing, it is to close your lips if you start in criticism. And if you need to, bite your tongue a couple of times to remind yourself that we're taking the light of understanding out of our auras when we stand in criticism.

At the time of Lent, I find myself giving up something in the name of overcoming my likes and dislikes. That's a Lenten privilege. And we might observe it. It's great what it does for a person just to observe that "I didn't even miss it!" It's not giving the things that we're through with, it's sharing the things we love that gets us into the state of illumination and development, that we may express within ourselves God's love, and exercise the soul to the point where we're receptive to all the Voice has given us. Your entire physical being has to be attuned to the hearing of it.

BARBARA I saw a ceiling of light; it was like you could look up at it through a skylight. I saw pale rose, blue, lavender, many of the pale colors mingled together touched by light. They were colors associated with the 7th Plane that appeared to deepen and have more meaning than ever before.

MARY You had gone through the Channel; that was just before you left the Channel to go to your night work. Going through the Channel at night through prayer, that is just about the coloring that you have as you go through. If that comes back as a memory, eventually you will see the door that goes into the other world. That's very good, Barbara. It would be well to note that, because many bring back that same vision.

BILL JACKSON After being at class, I saw streams of light coming up from the horizon into the sky.

MARY Yes. Hold that in your heart, and see if something more will be given.

MARGARET I received this: tall arches of light with tops bent inward in kind of a circle, as if it were a chapel with various towers and turrets.

GRACE Waking, I saw two guides from the Other Side encased in light. I saw them quite clearly. Their headdresses were Egyptian.

ESTHER ESTABROOK As I've sat here tonight, every time I close my eyes I see a shaft of pure bright light, like a star, just a shaft of light shining down that's like a magnet, and I have to draw back up toward it. What would that be?

MARY I would say that you're surrounded by love; the light of love is surrounding you.

*****

THE TEMPLE OF INCEPTION

Inception is a noun meaning entering, initiation, beginning an action. Jesus was a high initiate of the Essene disciples and learned all their mysteries.

In this Temple of Inception we are given the seven steps of initiation. These steps correspond to the seven sacred life centers in our bodies, also seven centers of force in the same region as the glands are located. The centers of force are in the etheric body of man; the ductless glands are in the dense physical body. The ductless glands are the points of contact between man's soul and his body.

The pituitary gland transforms energy into form. In the initiated one we see the twelve channel colors radiating throughout the channel, which reveals the spiritual status of the seeker.

All spiritual development is a matter of daily awareness, perseverance and faithfulness to truth. There is an age old teaching; first of all, it taught that the spirit of man is a ring of invisible fire, the birthless, deathless, immortal spark from the Infinite.

Now let us consider the light of a candle. Close to the wick is a glow nearly colorless; around it a ring of golden light; and still farther out, surrounding the yellow, is a deeper orange or reddish flame that gives off smoke. These three lights – blue, yellow, and red – are closely related to the flame of life in man. The blue, fuelless light represents the spirit. The yellow, giving no smoke, is the life and light of the mind. And the reddish glow is the sex fire, which the ancients called the consuming fire.

The ancients often spoke of these three fires within man as the fire of divinity, the fire of humanity, of culture and civilization, and fire of hatred, greed, and evil. In our spiritual arc colors, the arc of spiritual blue represents Training of the Ego; the arc of yellow represents Illumination; and the colors of the arc of red we name Metamorphosis.

MARGARET   Just before midnight, I was given a brilliant glimpse of the inside of part of this temple. Beautiful colored glass windows of rich sapphire blue dominated the arched walls, with a few touches of very bright color for contrast. The next morning I got the impression what I had seen was called the Chancel in the Chapel of the Windows of the Soul. This is the outer Chapel.

I see a row of slender pipes about sixteen feet high in a light golden beige color, bound together with a slender, darker band. On either aide is a large green leaf, curving outward. The teacher says, "They're your flute, your set of pipes on which to play your song of eternal life. The set is complete. Please use them. The range is magnificent." I feel grateful for the gift.

I am looking up into the inside of an infinitely tall tower lighted with shades of purples and violets, deep to pale. It is "the succession," made visible to me, the stepping down of power or inspiration from far higher realms, an inner view.

I am in a large circular room, later named The Audience Room or Inner Chapel. The walls are pale, vibrant rosy apricot. A design in deep relief like a rose window forms the floor. The framework or ribs are of the same rosy apricot or coral, lighter than the "Adoration" color. The spaces in between are pale blues, 11th and 12th of the Spiritual Blues.

I feel it is the wheel of life. I walk to the center and see my life laid out around me. Colors in sparkles rise from the floor. They are the essences of various emanations or personalities, and I feel good about it. As I watch, the floor, my wheel, seems to blend into one material, like a liquid cloth of this same delightful color.

A teacher invisible to me says: "It is the warp and woof of your life. Indissoluble. From it you may create anything you like, just so it is beautiful and true and therefore enduring." I remembered a starred crown of the same colors which had been given me several months ago. Instantly the crown is on my head, and I am robed in the whole of the beautiful fabric. The robe is weightless with no dragging from the past. No seams. I feel beautiful and know there is a beautiful radiance which I cannot see.

There at the center of myself, I immediately know that to rule myself is quite enough. My past lives are present in symbol and light. The teacher says: "You dare not sidestep the fruit of these previous, magnificent efforts." I am shown a large diamond shape. The session is clearly at an end.

******

THE TEMPLE OF INCARNATION UNIVERSAL

Upon entering the temple, we were taken to the Place of Records, where the keepers of the great scales of the universe take those of mankind who cannot themselves look into the past, and here they're shown those things that are reflected in their future, so that upon Earth they may know what of their own free will they must do to adjust the balance.

When we enter that great audience hall with its walls of smooth whiteness, we're allowed to see our progress in spiritual attainment. Some see it as a storehouse of clay tablets, and to others the records are carved upon sheets of gold or scribed in bright colors upon a vellum page; some see in the likeness of papyrus rolls or frescoes upon a temple wall. In whatever form seen, among the records there is one on which one sees one's true name, and none other can they read. When they hold it in their hands, they see what they must know for the hastening of their long journey, like a vision in a looking bowl, like sleep memory, yet clearer.

After leaving The Temple of Incarnation Universal, we were taken to a lesser temple, a sub-temple wherein all is melody. Here, amidst essence of sweet sound, the joy of hearing is intensified, and one can feel these splendid harmonies as water knows the urgent river's quest for foam capped mountains and tumultuous seas, and shares the mist of leisurely cascades and calm tranquility of pools beneath the moon. We hear the songs of mothers singing to bring their children sleep. The songs are sweet as the shadows of the warm scented dusk. Our hearts are filled with sympathy, and slow tears of grief become distilled until the sorrow of the world is caught up into a God given glistening sigh of summer rain.

And here are sweeping galaxies of sound which weave together intricate designs patterned with turquoise, violet, blue and rose, saffron, vermillion, amethyst and green, making a fabric of celestial song. Here is the source from whence all music flows. But only scattered silver drops reach Earth as liquid notes from strings of harp or lute, or bubbling from the night bird's trembling throat that stirs the perfume of sleeping flowers. We rejoiced; we were lost in a bewilderment of paths, and now we vowed to follow Christ, the winged one, to freedom. Bless you.

ANDREW   What is the Christ teaching? What is Christ Consciousness? I like to remind myself that aside from Jesus the man, what we mean by the Christ is that it refers to the light that each of us innately is – the self, Atman, the Buddha nature, the pearl of great price, the mustard seed that grew into a great tree. It's our core and our potential of becoming.

MIRIAM WILLIS Think of the vitalizing force of your own spirit body. The Christ repeatedly said to his disciples that which he had was theirs. He said we are not denied.

MARY We're refreshed as we go back and forth at night, revealing to our own souls the promises that were made at the time the Master walked the Earth, and we have a longing to share all these things we've seen there. In our dream life we recognize them. It's the opening of the soul revealing to the individual that God has a message for the person ready to receive it, who feels the result of touching the hand of the Master.

Christ does not come to reveal himself as a personality to you, but once hearing that Voice in the temple, you know that he has lived and that you are living in what he left behind. And as truly as I stand here and breathe before you, God is real; Christ is real; heaven is a perfected place. It's a world of organization and beauty. It holds out to every living human being the same Plan of Life, a plan of harmony and happiness if they have so accepted.

But nothing is forced upon anyone. God does not punish us nor does he take us by the hand and lead us, but he showed us through the Christ. Today the chaos in the world can be very quickly relieved if every man could find his portion of harmony within himself. And so we must learn first to respect ourselves and then respect the fact that we are a part of great God Almighty, who did send his son. And as the Tree of Life grows within us, we are nothing without that power that was given us at birth.

When God breathed into each soul the breath of life, he also gave us a role to play in life. Each one in his own way was to serve the Master. And the great Architect drew the plan upon our souls, if only we could read that Plan. And how do we do it? First, by believing, then by faithfully taking it upon ourselves.

Paul, the great narrator of our Christian religion, told us we had three bodies. We do so believe: physical, mental, and spiritual. But we find the spiritual body has been underused. It has been waiting there for us, and we haven't taken advantage of it. Faith is first. Remove the fear of not accomplishing. Faith is a thing of glory, of color. It is a winged thing. Capture it. Let it live with you and within you.

HELEN VON GEHR I've looked at the beautiful canvas Miriam painted that hangs over the organ thousands of times. Tonight for the first time I was struck with the light around the Christ. I kept meditating on that wonder, and it seemed that the light got brighter and brighter as I looked at it. I closed my eyes and thought, wouldn't it be wonderful if one saw the Christ light like Paul did on the Road to Damascus?

******

THE TEMPLE OF DIRECTION
BY THE ORDER OF ST. GABRIEL

As we enter the area surrounding the Temple in the Valley of the Pines, we see before us a credo which we are asked to read in unison. It reads thus: I believe that air-castles are emotional specifications to be crystallized into activity. Were we as plants with roots planted firmly in the soil of the earth, this might be impossible. But as our roots are sunk deeply and firmly in the ground of logic, reason, and intuition, nothing is impossible. And on these theories of facts I base my activities of common sense, not on powers of superstition.

And as there are no sins but mistakes, no sinners or saints unless we think it so, we have a right to our perspective of right and wrong. In my development of the Channel I must seek silence, and eventually I will know that spiritual birth follows with illumination; no speech is necessary. As speech is of time, silence is of eternity. We leave the Temple, a symbol of man's search for light, and now enter a pathway winding through shining lands, through wild groves of untouched sycamores.

We see ahead of us the shining one, waiting to give us his message, Thou whom Christ loves, awaiting the call to the Eightfold Path, walk forth in pure untrammeled love. Never withdraw from a soul in distress, nor trouble a soul with words of self; address thyself to God, seek not self-satisfaction. The wind of my music is blowing through the soul. Listen to the chords of the inner sphere playing in the heart, removing desire to be noticed as the singer. As thou art willing to sink the instrument in my love, the music soars into the realms of spirit, adding its voice to the celestial choirs. See the humble son of God, enter the temple. He also opens the hidden door of the soul. Bless you, Mary.

MARGARET   In meditation I experienced the fission of a fountain. I saw a light green forest of new growth with trees on the right. I could see the path plainly and went there quickly. The trees became grey. They had sucked power from us. Then I came upon a darker green forest. The path was not so clear, but I was given more strength to see it. Then at a seashore, I watched ships. We knelt to pray on the shore. A towel was given me, thrown across my knees. It contained writing that I couldn't read. I saw a dark mirror. We were all asked the question: "What have you done with your lives?"

MIRIAM WILLIS Saint Gabriel was the one who announced the coming of the Christ. He brought the message of the gift of the Christ within, the balancing of the human and divine. If you notice, these fourteen spirals are double, "7" being a mystical number.

ANDREW   I'm interested in St. Gabriel being head of the 7th Plane.

MARY   This happens to be the Hierarchy of St. Gabriel; this temple is under their control. You'll find many bits of information will come through that band that we don't get from any other band. There's a great healing force that goes with the band. People have said to me, I'm on the 15th plane now but I've never enjoyed anything more than the 7th.   When we get to the 8th Plane and we're on the Eightfold Path, a great deal is recorded that we must remember. So let us have the pleasure of living with this band on the 7th Plane while we can.

ANDREW This is the first time I've heard of Gabriel being referred to as a saint - an archangel can be a saint?

MARY Yes, St. Michael the Archangel is also a saint. It is so in the Heaven world. Usually the archangels are lifted to a position in the order where they are sainted. They have a power and an influence. They are workers, masters, or have attained a great many other virtues. Those that are trained in the Christis Band are nearly always later used over quite a populace, a number of people that are developing on that side of life.

VIOLET We often get messages from the Band of St. Gabriel.

MARY As I presented you to the Hierarchy one by one, they were very much pleased. As those twelve teachers stood there and looked at our group carrying their auras with light in them and the colors that we fashioned through thinking Color first, then applying the brush to the aptitude of our minds, we change the chemistry of our body to where it reflects us, what we think, how we live.

We also had some poisonous colors, and they washed clean. When these colors first appeared to you, your auras were seeped in primitive colors, so you could see the change between last year and this year.

JEANNE I think I had an experience exactly what you're talking about, where I was in a room, and I did see a painting, and I knew it had something to do with me. There were a lot of ugly colors in the canvas. Then a teacher came and washed the red plum color of spiritual wisdom, the 5th ray of Spiritual Purple, and some other very beautiful colors over it.

As I watched, it seemed like the painting was washed with water, and I thought, oh no, don't take those beautiful colors away! But then, in other words, it was as if the colors had been given on purpose to that painting to change it, and then with the water, everything washed away like a water color, and what was left was a beautiful impression underneath. When I looked closer at it, I saw there were three different views of my face. It was a very illuminating feeling, having seen this.

MARY You faced illumination of yourself.

MIRIAM ALBPLANALP Could you tell us more about when you took us before the Hierarchy?

MARY We went in. We stood there and were examined, and as we walked through, they told us whether we had made improvements. We didn't hear what they said to the person beside us; the words were for each person only. And you'd be surprised how many times they said, "Try not to be so self centered." That's one of the things that was meant for all. I can understand it, because we're all doing the best we can do, and we're all so interested in trying to do the right thing by everybody else, that it's what we do, is it not? Sometimes that makes or breaks the day.

So, I think they had that understanding, but they realized that we would have more pleasure in life if we'd withdraw from the critical analysis of ourselves and others. That seems to be what they're trying to break into our consciousness. If only we could look at ourselves and say, as happy as I am, I'm going to try to be a bit different from now on.

But to live and see the same fault over and over again in a person, how can the person ever become released from that fault?

ANDREW Special urns I saw last week were from the Temple of Holiness, a sub-temple of the Temple of Direction.

HELEN VON GEHR I had a vision in which, looking at a delicate flower, I saw there a face, then a white peacock. Then the peacock assumed beautiful colors. Then I saw a teacher in a white robe with red borders. This reminded me of the "Christ knocking at the door" picture. I felt that Christ does go with us on the Eightfold Path.

RALPH Is there anything we should be doing now, to be prepared for the Eightfold Path?

MARY Write out what you think you've done to change your life. This is not a confessional; this is a witness to change. It's wonderful.

******

THE TEMPLE OF REINCARNATION
IN THE TOWER OF SOUL

MARGARET I see opalescent pearly white reflecting all colors. Doors are of mother-of-pearl. Inside, the halls are painted in the colors of the inner channel of our being, since it is within this channel that the seed atom of the soul is lodged, through this channel that we are reborn, and by this channel that we return to spirit.

ESTHER BARNES   Here, one who is ready to reincarnate is taken to prepare him for his sojourn on Earth. Here he learns what the plan of his life will be and the soul takes up his new life. The final decision is made for the time of rebirth into the earth; preparations ensue, and many visits are made here prior to the actual rebirth itself. With permission, we may go here to read from what was given from the Akashic records, in order to talk over with our heavenly teachers gleanings from our past lives and decisions for our future ones.

There are many fountains and bathing spas on the grounds surrounding this temple; there are many water tests here to cleanse the emotions before unadulterated decisions can be made. For each test, one is accompanied by a teacher who discusses the test with the person. After the test, it's determined whether or not the cleansing is complete, and whether or not further testing of the soul's emotions is needed.

We reincarnate with the desire to evolve, and even when it seems we're not making progress, we really are, simply by undergoing life's experiences. We learn through hardship, failure and mistakes even more than through our successes and triumphs.

MIRIAM ALPLANALP   With regard to reincarnation, if you were having a lesson in this temple, how do they do it? Suppose you have ten lives to look at and talk about. How exactly do they illustrate it?

MARY It's illustrated. They pick first one life and then another life, and put balance there. They break down your life and your thinking, and they pick it up universally and see how your thinking would affect the people you're with, as an example.

MIRIAM ALBPLANALP You mean we each went through that when we visited this temple?

MARY We each review pictures in the temples. Get familiar with them. Remember, we use our spiritual eyes. We're especially accountable for criticism. Criticism is one of the things that tears down this structure of ours.

****

THE TEMPLE OF EVES

MIRIAM WILLIS Those of mankind who are able to travel the heights approach the Temple of the Eves from every angle. The temple stands upon a high prominence and is considered to be a temple of intangibles. It appeared to me like a great angel, yet without form except that it had a left wing and a right wing. These are full of light and of rainbow colors in the most delicate tints that reach out to us. As these colors envelop us, they lift and cleanse us of earth vibrations, empowering us to go forward into the great temple.

These colors are also accompanied by the music of their essence, for every color exudes a tone and every tone a color. And as we enter the temple, drawn to the particular of the many entrances that we are attracted to, we find within it a great light and a circular altar of gold centered in a great dome-like room.

We file from right to left in a spiral ascendance and take our places without being directed, just through the vibratory action of knowing the appropriate spot to reach. Everyone seems to sway a little to the soft music playing. Presently the music stops. We are still. A silence descends upon us, a silence full of fragrance, a silence that seems so deep and wide and high that it embraces our entire consciousness. A ruby studded communion cup is passed.

We hear the voice of the Great One. We are privileged to go alone into an inner sanctum to repeat our vows. We are so thankful for the magnificent supply that is never lacking to those who seek. We now climb that lighted passage of our being in the inner Channel to receive the inflow of power and new life. And with this thought we experience an overflow of love. All the most glorious color rays are bestowed upon us, showering over us, in and through us.

DALE I saw a temple of the 12th of blue and the yellow color of enlightenment. The gates were a misty blue, the steps were the pink lavender of the color of inspiration leading to a purple door. In huge room, there were many beveled mirrors, each one containing reflected colors. I saw my own colors in a mirror at the end of the room and merged into it. The mirrors leave their essence, as one is in rapport with the inspiration he receives. I think this was a test of faith and perseverance.

PATTI I've been thinking how wonderful it is for so many people to want the spiritual life, who believe in living in eternity now, one world without end, amen. It's such a blessing and a gift to be in a room where many people all share this, all want to live good lives, all want to do right, spread love.

******

THE TEMPLE OF DEVOTION

VIOLET From messages received from the Brotherhood: Seven spirals lead us to the Temple of Devotion, where we see seven circular staircases. Seven steps lead to each staircase. Each staircase trains one in concentration, purpose, intent, desire, goals, and faith. Each stair is of a different color. These colors are: blue, pinkish mauve, orange, orange red, golden, delphinium blue, greens in basic to nile, and deep purple.

One has to choose which staircase to ascend first, as the staircases are not marked. Choice is made by feeling the vibrations. The stairways are ascended on successive nights. The topmost one is in a circular room. There, one is given lessons in vibration.

MIRIAM ALBPLANALP Regarding the tests we took this week, Jeanne was speaking of circles, and although I don't exactly recall circles, if I could describe an increasing feeling this week, it would be one of rounded fullness.

MARY Well, another person said they saw a series of crystal balls that took on the different colors. The very last ball seemed to be made of plastic rather than anything heavy. When they reached out to try to touch it, the balls began to lift as balloons that became spiritual thoughts that were placed into space to be absorbed. After a while, those balloons seemed to flow out a little gas, an essence, something very pleasant to smell, that was a developing chemical that was given you on that side.

So these circles contain quite a number of things, and the test was whether you recognized that these circles were for you and that you should appreciate them. Then, when the essence came and you observed it, you saw the little "puff." When you breathed it in, you were exhilarated.

******

PART II

THE PLATEAU BETWEEN

THE 7TH AND 8TH PLANES

MAP OF THE PLATEAU
BETWEEN
THE 7TH AND 8TH PLANES

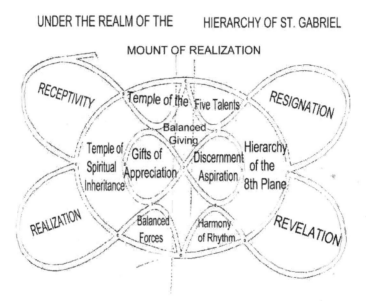

UNDER THE REALM OF THE   HIERARCHY OF ST. GABRIEL

MOUNT OF REALIZATION

RECEPTIVITY   Temple of the Five Talents   RESIGNATION

Balanced Giving

Temple of Spiritual Inheritance Gifts of Appreciation Discernment Aspiration Hierarchy of the 8th Plane

REALIZATION   Balanced Forces Harmony of Rhythm   REVELATION

PLATEAU BETWEEN 7TH AND 8TH PLANES

THE PLATEAU BETWEEN THE 7TH AND 8TH PLANES
HIERARCHY OF ST. GABRIEL

MIRIAM WILLIS   Let us clothe ourselves in our keynote color and be arrayed in it. All of us need faith, so we'll wrap the cloak of faith about us and line it with whatever color you want or feel the need of. Now let us rest easily and comfortably, with our body in alignment with the inflow of God's loving grace and power. May we have no slightest block or anything to deter in any way, or to cross the vibrations. Let us relinquish anything that is restless or disturbing.

In this simple way, we have raised each portion of our being, the three bodies, by the infilling of the holy breath and the integration of the whole in balance and in beautiful color. Let us feel through our imagination and the spirit's revealing the great reality of this which we have learned to venerate, which builds within ourselves the real respect for that which God has created in so mysterious and wonderful a way for ourselves and everyone who walks the earth, for those who realize it and for those who do not yet realize anything beyond their own mental processes.

And let us know that they will come again, or perhaps in this life there will come to them a great awakening. And now let us think a moment of our own awakening. There have been so many on this road, seeking, traveling ever onward toward illumination, dwelling within the focus and the ease and comfort of enlightenment. Oh what treasures we already have had.

We're starting a Plateau that carries with it a consciousness that is absolutely unique. After having visited all the temples of the 7th Plane, seven night classes were spent in the testing of the 7th Plane before entering the silence in preparation for the 8th Plane on the Plateau. So much takes place on this Plateau between the 7th and 8th Planes.

We stand with the realization that we are individuals created to use self will and creative energy. We can go to the heights or to the depths. What would be a pitfall? If we have much, and we go on expecting that that will continue being given us. We must earn the right.

The seeker enters from the right side. At the top of the Plateau are scales to which one has climbed. It's been a long upward way. Here one pivots, weighs what has been revealed in development, and recognizes the need to be resolved in deeper understanding. Here at the top of the Plateau, we're told what we've done and left undone. On the way down we're told what the Eightfold Path holds for us.

MARY When the inner marriage takes place, we have to be aware of the habitual things we do every day. It's living on a path of not seeing the fault in another, or we recognize the fault and allow them to keep the fault without criticism. They are living with it, and so can we. Tolerance comes when the soul recognizes its placement in the sight of God.

MIRIAM WILLIS This Plateau between the 7th and 8th Planes is shaped like a figure eight, the meaning of which is union and togetherness. It holds the record of the element which is its nourishment, the Christ teaching. The Plateau represents hidden life, the within that is real, darkness surrounded by cleansing waters. Color guides the seeker through the hidden channel of darkness to the light. The silence of love and peace lies within, a well of knowledge to be drawn upon when needed. True freedom comes to fruition here.

On the Plateau, we find:

1. TEMPLE OF REVELATION — Here we see in mirrors our growth, lacks and limitations, to determine if we have attained enough power to go on to the 8th Plane. This is the revealing to the seeker the reality of his growth, a true picture of his attainment of selfless love, the power of God within him functioning through him.

2. TEMPLE OF HARMONY OF RHYTHM - Here we are strengthened in perfect rhythm and tone. Harmony of rhythm is exactly like learning to dance: it requires exercise and polishing.

It will strengthen with use in perfect rhythm and tone into Balanced Forces.

3. TEMPLE OF BALANCED FORCES This opaline blue temple holds the promise of spiritual sight and hearing. Forces here are fine tuned more perfectly than our earthly forces. When our three bodies are balanced, we find greater poise and grace. Emotions have been cleansed; one is at peace with oneself and one's brother.

4. THE AREA OF REALIZATION We realize the benefits already received and practiced; we realize what we have become.

5. TEMPLE OF DISCERNMENT and ASPIRATION — A high goal with high hopes to be able to recognize weakness and strengths. Growth in the faculties of discernment and aspiration must become established within the soul and function with ease through the spiritual body.

6. TEMPLE OF GIFTS OF APPRECIATION deepens respect for the greatness of God's gifts of power and fullness which one has been able to assimilate into his being.

7. TEMPLE OF SPIRITUAL INHERITANCE Here he receives an initiation, the inheritance of all his attainments in soul development up to this degree of growth. We inherit the riches of that which we have gained.

8. TEMPLE OF RECEPTIVITY or Expansion of Spiritual Faculties to the degree that one can continue development on the Eightfold Path, 8th Plane.

9. TEMPLE OF FIVE TALENTS: We are tested here on the inner development of the counterpart of the five senses. The Temple of the Five Talents comprises the spiritual counterpart of the five physical senses of sight, hearing, smell, touch, taste.

10.   TEMPLE OF BALANCED GIVING: Tested on service to others, and what we have attained of giving the self up to the 7th Plane for entree to the 8th Plane.

11. TEMPLE OF RESIGNATION: Area for those who have not made the grade required. They receive special training to try again to make the grade with others.

****

THE AREA OF BALANCED REALIZATION

Balanced Realization is comprised of two large areas at the top of the 7th Plane, one to the right and one to the left of the Hierarchy of St. Gabriel, which is the controlling power of this Plateau. The seeker frequents these areas many times, going back and forth to be tested, to recall and experience teachings which help to balance forces, empower and clarify revelations, and cleanse the seeker for entrance to the Eightfold Path.

The buildings here are set in beautiful gardens with spacious lawns and many varieties of trees. There is beauty and restfulness everywhere. One is impressed by the perfect symmetry and balance of design. One can readily find secluded places to ponder beside a cool river or near one of the many fountains. Here one learns the all-encompassing truth of the two great commandments given by Jesus: to love God with all one's heart, soul, mind and strength, and to love one's neighbor as oneself.

One is especially impressed with the necessity of applying these commandments to all the details of daily living. In the initiations experienced for acceptance to the Eightfold Path, there is a similarity for each soul, yet differing in emphasis according to need. It is the nature of the universe to give us what we're able to take. There comes to each seeker the logical and exact result of his own receptivity.

Here is a time of rest, of absorption of the rhythms of life, color and music, as these are all contained within the protection of the sacred inner being that is insulated from the world. The seeker comes to the end of himself; the very depths and heights of his being are explored with a poignancy of reality that carries him into a labyrinth of darkness and light, where he faces defeats and victories to the theme of constant desire, of hunger and thirst.

One experiences the whole of his inner life, though he has not journeyed forth nor moved from his place in a great antechamber. When weariness possesses him, immediately appear before him refreshing nectars and a couch to support him. The atmosphere glows with rose amber rays of strength which renews and fills his soul with peace.

The seeker rises, poised and balanced in a stillness of bliss beyond words, as though his life had been swept clean. His hunger and thirst are quenched. He is expectant, knowing there is much still to be experienced requiring all his balanced forces in surrender.

When one desires to follow the Path, truth is revealed which keeps one centered. With the color of faith surrounding one and going within, wisdom will be given. Courage will guide you and life will be balanced as you follow the Eightfold Path.

******

THE TEMPLE OF REALIZATION

MARY As the Plateau of Balanced Realization emphasizes man's search within for a greater understanding of himself, so the Temple of Realization on the Plateau presents the other side of the picture, the dawning and deepening realization of his Creator.

As we enter this temple, we're amazed at the amount of silence between ourselves and God. We stand in the great hall of silence, and with the forces about us, we realize that nothing has been denied. The circumstances of our lives have come as a warring force. We went with the force. We ceased to be creative because we didn't go the way we should.

People who've been successful often have a hard time taking advice, because once they've climbed that hill of success, it's a mountain of consciousness to get over it, to mend bridges when they've been washed out. I have known many people who suffered great losses. I've known the unworthy that have had so much gain during the life that they hardly had the use of it.

I've known those that reached the top, as it were, and suddenly they were reduced. And on our social service list are many people with magnificent possibilities if they had the chance. The chance does not seem to come to them. I ask you why? In this Temple of Realization, if that has happened to us, we learn why we've had reverses or advantages, why we've failed and where we've succeeded. We're trying to gain the balance of our soul's worth, to know the visions that come are given to us for our benefit.

Is God is pointing the finger of life another way for you? If you're unsuccessful in the spot you're now in, right about face and say, "Direct me, because I'm willing to be directed." In the Temple of Realization, we realize if we can relinquish our egos long enough to listen. The spiritual ear never becomes deaf, the spiritual eyes always see. So we strive harder to overcome, and in overcoming, there's that healing ray of enlightenment in the living in Color and having the purple of faith about you.

Wednesday night as we waited there over there, we were one unit of people seeking the same thing, quietly saying thank you over and over. We didn't need voices; thankfulness was in the breath we drew, all trying to communicate thanks to the Father and his son as the holy guardians of our lives, the invisible helpers and teachers that grant us the privilege of knowing them in these temples. It was in the very element about us that you were risen above and so privileged to be there. It's hard to describe to you.

When I try to put things in words, they seem so idle sometimes to me, to try to impart what we have there. If we go back to the thought of what we have, our hands are overflowing and we can always take time to share. As you went to the temple the night before, if you could have brought with you that wonderful serenity.

VIOLET   At the Temple of Realization, we ascend very wide steps of green porphyry with water running gently over them. I seem to be with my husband, who is over in that world. Feeling deeply in sympathy with each other, we ascend hand in hand. Three steps lead us into an interior of great beauty, yet not vast. The walls are of green malachite. We walked the length of the temple and knelt at the far end before a very plain altar of what seemed like emerald.

A light radiates from this altar so that it glows with marvelous brilliance, and a gentle yet authoritative voice speaks. It says, "Beloved seekers after truth, you are trained and sent forth that you may serve those in need. It is a healing mission to loosen, to release, and this you have pledged yourselves to do.

"And so we are bidden as messengers of the Lord, for you do this in his name. In this great name of power we bless you. Go forth and serve." Then the Voice ceased. We arose and departed. Our feet seemed to be as though they had wings, and our hearts were as eagles, because we were lifted up in power and sent forth.

This is being born again. Jesus referred to the "consciousness of the Christ in you." The saving of the soul of man comes through aligning his soul with the perfection and purpose of the divine plan of life, for the spirit is the essence of divinity and its attributes are of its own choosing. All is within the will. Upon these choices lies the future, whether it be toward darkness or light. The whole hierarchy of those who shine in the realm of infinite wisdom and inestimable power is available to your spirit for salvation and peace.

LOLA   Around the Temple of Realization is a mist of the many purple colors of the Scale of Love plume. The temple itself is transparent crystal, its roof projecting farther out than the walls. The walls are the color of the brilliant rose fuscia color of sympathetic understanding, the 7th ray of the Spiritual Arc of Purple. To each was given his own light.

ESTHER BARNES   I had something from the Temple of Realization about column forces. It was the vision of an eight columned classic Greek temple facing west to the sunset. I knew it was facing west because there was a glorious sunset glow on it. The color of the 11th of spiritual purple, that beautiful rose bisque of grace, was particularly noticeable. Everything was bathed in opalescent light.

MARGARET   I received a message from the Temple of Realization on how to tune in to one's keynote color via the heavenly lute, with urging to do it for ourselves.

JEANNE I gazed through a mist to see the colors of the Scale of Love plume, especially the colors of the rose fuscia of sympathetic understanding and the blue plum, depth of love color of the 3rd color of spiritual purple.

The temple facade was crystal in the twelve glowing shades of the Spiritual Arc of Purple, and at the same time, it looked to me as if the temple's outer walls had been rubbed. Underneath was a pink color of aspiration and over that were the purples. The temple's inside walls glistened with mica or a jewel like substance in colors of rose and the Arc of Spiritual Green rays. Circles of light were spinning like Saturn's rings outside a chamber door. Inside, a sanctuary had similar spinning circular Saturn-like rings. Outside this temple, I saw what was called the Tree of Health. This tree bore both fruit and flowers.

MARGARET From this temple, I've been receiving messages on the lions.

MARY There are so many; the list is long. It's good to keep track, to recognize these faults in yourselves. One fault seldom recognized is impatience with ourselves and other people. It takes a long time to kill that lion.

MIRIAM WILLIS   As we recognize these lions, we then temper the ego from lion to lamb.

MARY The lions are your habits, your secret little sins, humoring yourself, your set opinions, the jealousies you don't even recognize, the vanities. It's too bad when we let down our guard to not do what we can. You can receive help for dispositional traits and be reminded of those that you need to overcome. Test yourself. See if you can realize it as a part of the night work.

MIRIAM WILLIS The lion, the mightiest of beasts, is in all religions. Very few beasts can overcome the lion. We liken these faults of ours to a lion. They're in the lower consciousness.

MARY   We become annoyed. These annoyances break down the chemical forces. Like a fine spider web, we keep spinning. After a while this chemical change takes place; these strands that we have been spinning gradually change us.

MIRIAM WILLIS   Here are some practical things we come to realize in the Temple of Realization:

Right belief, right aspirations that lead to right attitudes toward others' beliefs, and that lead to wisdom;

Right speech: to speak only in kindness, with love, with words of encouragement and helpfulness.

Right conduct in every area: to behave in sincerity, simplicity and grace. Thoughtful consideration of others at all times.

Right effort: moderate in all things, respect for self and all men. Fair minded in all transactions

Right mindedness: anticipating needs of others; to discriminate between our needs and our wants. To seek mental maturity, the control of our thoughts.

Right livelihood, that each shall carry his own responsibility. Choose a right mode of earning that has honest, thrifty ways.

Right meditation: to enter into reality through meditation. To plumb the depths and soar the heights. To find balance for life until the Christ within becomes the master, and we become his willing servants.

MARY Miriam is giving you the headings of many a lecture you've listened to on the Other Side. That's an explanation of the path as you climb. They're very difficult to read off that way and just take them as a bitter dose. That's about what you received in the temples. When we've been in a temple and heard this, we believe this is possible. You come out thinking I'm able to do that if I just apply myself, because you've been in a vibration that has enlivened you to the thought that anything is possible with God. We do feel that.

We've been trying to get together on it, realize what's possible, because one of the things that's hardest for us to do is to bring this spiritual realization into our active lives. Hold what you've been given over there and see if you can't realize your training from there. Having me to tell you won't do you any good. If you can reveal it to yourself, you'll realize that each time you go there, as you're tested and given the rights to the temple, then you have something you can bank on.

Oh dear Father, receive the loving humility of my heart. I open it up to thee that thou mayest fill it with thy divine power that, refreshed, I may again pick up my load, be it easy or hard. Thy beloved son will be my true companion and thy whole spirit my guide, so I shall go ever forward and upward, having confidence that I am ever climbing upward to thee. Amen.

****

THE TEMPLE OF REVELATION

To our left, we enter the Temple of Revelation. We have entered the Creative Color Channel. We have climbed the ladder in divine consciousness and received direction in a burst of divine illumination.

This is what our master called being born again. He said the consciousness of the Christ mind must be in you. He also said, I am nothing if I am not the savior of the world, but the saving is of the soul of man, and that comes only through the aligning of his soul with the perfection and the purpose of the divine plan of life.

For the spirit is of the essence of divinity and all its attributes are of its own choosing. Nothing is forced upon it. All is within the will of man.

MARGARET I've been conscious of a new dimension in prayer, also a new constant awareness of sin in my life. By sin, I mean this in the sense of the translation of the word 'sin' from the Greek, meaning misperception. For the first time in relation to my attitude toward people who were antagonistic toward me, I began to feel love for those who are in darkness. I had a sense of identification with people who were suffering, a new dimension coming from the darkness. I have had this feeling of love since Sunday morning.

MARY Then you've had a revelation. Something was revealed to you.

****

THE TEMPLE OF ASPIRATION

CLARA I'm first aware of a pale blue expanse diminishing into an area of new grasses, dotted with tiny flowers like the new grasses of spring after the rain. Next I'm going down a very neat path with high shrubs and foliage along the sides. The bushes look like a type of hibiscus, but later I found them to be roses of Sharon.

Next I start passing under white and lavender latticed arches along the path. Soon the path forks and in the center is a raised grassy expanse. I'm next aware of walking through an entrance with huge arches overhead. The walls are a silvery grey with a pearlescent quality cut like stone. Inside there is a huge room where the walls seem to let the light through, not completely, but as in a beautiful silvery ray. The inside area is so large that the people moving around below are very small in comparison. Now everyone is standing in loose flowing garments of soft smoky colors.

The inside area is full of beautiful silvery rays. The people are arranged as though they're sitting in pews, although they're standing. Everything blends in, like a cross between a black pearl and a mother of pearl.

There's a teacher in the center wearing white garments. He is aglow. The teacher looks something like the picture of Jesus at a doorway. As I stand and listen it is as if all my consciousness is directed upon him. There's a circular light about his being from his waist up it just glows so much I can't see his features any longer. As he talks, a lighted being is as if between him and me - my consciousness is lifted up and I'm not aware of anything else. It seems as if there are lighted beams between him and me as he speaks.

MARY What a beautiful paper. It's wonderful Clara. We're so grateful. I wish you'd try to go on and write more. I see you can get more.

CLARA It seemed like there was a hallway too. Is there a hallway with statues on the side, gold on the arches?

MARY Yes, that's right. The end of the 7th Plane.

CLARA In the hall there's a high up ceiling, but there are lower arches. There is thick gold on it. There are statues all the way up to the ceiling, spaced about three feet apart. At the end of the hall I encountered a crowned person of some kind. The walls were white and gold crinkled quartz. The decorative statues at first seemed Egyptian. I was inside a big pink pearlescent room made of thick rock, but light came through the rock.

MARGARET Faith took on new meanings for me recently, multiplying itself in scope, dimension and depth, until I suddenly felt I knew much more of what life is about. This is a summary of several of the experiences. When I realized intensely that all persons and things are one through the God in each, I was released from a heaviness caused by trying too hard to feel a sense of brotherhood with difficult persons.

The corollary is that I must feed good with faith, hold to that faith and know it will not fail. A second corollary is that I must nourish faith in myself: faith in my ability to receive trustworthy guidance and discrimination. At the same time I received this enlarged, enlivened concept of faith, I felt that every cell of my body was filled with new energy.

As I became alive to the bringing faith out of the shadows of vague intangibles and investing every detail of daily life with it, I felt the impact of faith on every segment of the Channel, seeing the permutations and combinations of inflections were endless and ever changing. I have experienced again and again the results of acting in faith on the promises given through Spirit. When my energies and attention are focused on a single goal at a time, the mists fall away, solutions to impossible problems appear out of nowhere, and I'm permitted to glimpse the golden interiors of human hearts.

Jesus said, "Thy faith hath made thee whole." I felt that sentence applied to me. I realize that wholeness has to be maintained, that one dose of faith is no more permanent than one lung full of air, but that the supply is unlimited. It seemed to me that the Channel, beginning with faith, ended with faith extended to peace; that faith extending as far as possible reaches the peace that passeth understanding. I experienced a rebuilding by feeling currents of faith flow through me. A willingness to let this happen made it possible.

Fear sometimes glues my joints, constricts my diaphragm and congeals my blood. I hope to remember to swim in faith in its all-embracing depths every day as if I were amphibious, knowing that when I emerge and go with the flow, the Font of Supply will meet my every need, and I will be enabled to fulfill my destiny.

Faith has become for me, through the study of Color and the night teaching in the temples, a living substance. It is the love for Christ, first of all, that inspired faith in me. Then I wanted to help those who had needs which, in turn, meant that I had to have the Faith to believe that Christ could work through me; first to heal me and make me a more fit vessel for his use; then to use me as a channel of love and healing for others. The faith that he would do it and that he was guiding me led me here to my teachers, into the conscious living in two worlds and into a life where the faith substance was transmuted into realities that I could see and touch.

Faith that they will speak to me and guide me has become their words, written down or spoken aloud, and sometimes their faces before my spiritual vision. Faith in the other side of life has become remembered experiences on the Other Side, in temples and among the beauties of heaven's world. Faith in thinking it possible to overcome negative dispositional traits has become a progressive reality in my life and lives of those for whom I pray, in color.

Faith in the power of healing prayer has become manifestations of healing in the lives of those prayed for. Faith in the great brotherhood of Christ has become the most real truth in my life. For I have been led, a step at a time, by faith and love, on the Pathway that brought me here to the teachers that make these realities possible.

****** *

THE TEMPLE OF RECEPTIVITY

MARY In the Temple of Receptivity, we are taught the seeking of divine adjustment or the miracle of living. In the living of the Christ way, "he leads us on by-paths we do not know." The seeker finds within his mind an abiding desire to know the future, to see around the corner of days and years. Even when it doesn't concern him about what will happen next month or next year, the insistence still remains. Our seeker wants to know.

If only we could be sure that all would be well; if we could have some guarantee that our present hopes would not betray us, leaving us deserted and lonely, then we would find peace and contentment. Life is not like that. The future is never quite a thing apart from all that has gone before. We bring into the present ingredients and cargoes from the past, and these are with us as we take the unknown path. All we have learned, felt and thought, all our experiences from birth to now, all the love that nourished us at other times, all the yearning rooted in our spirits, all are with us as we move into the unknown. For he leads us on by paths we do not know.

We enter this Temple of Receptivity with the normal feeling of anxiety which we face on the threshold of any new adventure. We were tested on strength of desire, on endurance, on ability to overcome hardships and to persevere. Each soul was his own judge and was able to measure to what degree he had developed these qualities, and how much further he needed to work on them.

We were shown many things of our past in sensory detail and became very conscious of the fullness of the life we've led. Things we may have missed at the time were exposed. For example the texture of the grass, the voice of a loved one unheard for many years. We were able to see that person standing as they were in the scene as it was, the sky as it was, even the wind the same. Only in this temple, the sensory details were heightened and the picture more vivid and meaningful.

We were allowed to live as the person we truly are for awhile. Then we were given an experience showing specifically where and how one slides and slips, reverting to the old everyday person we are used to being. What a difference!

Once you've entered this Temple, you are never the same. It leaves an indelible impression in knowing what belongs to you and how much inheritance awaits you. What you have earned becomes clear. You are aware of the magnification of benefits and full of desire to set the benefits gained into action.

JEANNE   High above me was a huge dome, which beams in light energy sparkling like diamonds. These particles of light are absorbed by us; all around the air vibrates with this energy, which is then transferred into chunks of the 11th and 12th of blue. The walls of the temple are magnetic; walking close to them, their energy is absorbed into you. In the very act of breathing one's breath manifests beautiful colors: glowing message bearer, depth of love, 12th of red, sympathy--great blocks of roses and the arc of purple colors appear before one's eyes, and there is a clarity of meaning.

The great hall is very tall and resembles a diamond cathedral; stalagmites and stalactites of beautiful designs shimmer everywhere, their surfaces reflecting all colors. Another large room is entirely of blue; this room seems dimensionless—the walls, the ceiling and air all flow into each other and are of one substance--- the 11th of spiritual blue with streaks of darker blue, having the quality of expansion and limitlessness.

At the same time, my line of vision encompassed an area of about 50 by 100, and 50 feet high, yet I felt the room to be much larger. After the experience in this room, one approaches an incline below which is a pool composed entirely of human tears. One cries into this pool tears for a person or experience not properly appreciated or understood in one's past. After having been cried into this pool, the tears lose their colorless state and are transformed into jewel-like colors of turquoise, sapphire, 9th and 10th of blue. At a later visiting, the waters contained a patch of self-revelation as well. It was understood that these tears held the promise of joy.

****

TEMPLE OF THE FIVE SENSES

The temple is right in the very heart of the figure eight. Beneath it is the Vale of Prayer.

VIRGINIA ANDERSON Tiny drops of light on soaring arches and clouds as a floor were a surprise to me. I could look up to the pale yellow of the temple pillars and then up to the rosy arches made of diffused light like a fog, with violet tones blended through toward the top. These last tones blended further into the sky. There was no ceiling. Where the arches merged, it was all sky. I was all alone, wondering how one could stand there on nothing but vapor for a floor.

******

THE TEMPLE OF THE FIVE TALENTS

MARY This is the temple of the human body, the greatest living thing God could create. These five senses are given us. We can enlarge on them. One person might say he became an artist, painted great pictures, planned great buildings. We get credit for all these senses over there in this temple. We are speaking of the human body and what it means, what it is capable of.

Try to share all you can of what you've proven to yourself. Do not take what I say, prove it for yourself and give it to someone else. We're fortunate when we share, when someone will tolerate what we know. I have watched people develop. When you're all alone, it's much more difficult to develop than when you have someone you can share with. That's truth; it's provable.

JEANNE I saw a curved stone structure. The curve was of a rare metal that shines with a brilliant intensity. Inside, one room is sky blue and sparkles as though there's something convex behind it. There's a hall with a white marble floor and a winding staircase heaped with flowers on the railing. We were shown a room of sensing where our senses were quickened to knowing we possess far more than we've dreamed.

At one point, having sailed through the royal purple of faith and the turquoise of the 9th ray of spiritual blue, we were quickly borne through etheric mists to another area. To each has been given many avenues of expression.

****

THE TEMPLE OF RESIGNATION

In the Chamber of Acceptance, one is prepared to take that which is his very own, accepting the assets and infirmities he has inherited. This enabling power envelops him in color and he sees the causes of his riches and his poverty.

Thus clad, he enters the Temple of Resignation, where his understanding is quickened in the realization that only as he is pledged to the truth of his being can he go forward, taking his responsibility and using fully that which he is, building on this foundation of truth toward the fulfillment of his aspirations. He realizes the uniqueness of himself and discovers the true foundation upon which his destiny evolves in day to day giving over to the creative power of love in active submission to his divine self, if he would gain entrée to the Eightfold Path.

This temple is of grey lavender shot through with glowing peach, rose, and blue, reaching high in activity that seems to fill with spiritual imagination all who will accept it.

******

THE BALANCED FORCES OF POWER

MARY Through Color and through faith that you're having revealed to you what is that next world, what have you learned about it? What has been given you? What have you brought back and given back? What have you over there in your safety deposit box in comparison to what you have here?

Too often we send over so little that's worthwhile, but oh, once in a while there's something that goes over that I'm sure even the angels smile upon, where someone makes a real sacrifice, and they're happy in the sacrifice. I think to be happy in the gift is the thing we have to learn, and not fear.

Many people give gifts and some give lavishly, but at the same time they're counting the cost, and they have an actual fear that they've gone too far. Search yourself. Did you make a pledge that's more than you can handle? Did you do it through vanity?

What is the shading between what we have that's ours and what we have that should be shared with others? The balancing of the forces is the thing that causes us to become selfless, because we're not in fear and we're not worrying about our expenditures.

If we have faith in climbing the Channel bringing a sense of development, we have gained something. When you really apply this to you daily living it becomes the breath of life. Put the purple of faith on and go forth. Unless you apply the principles it doesn't work. I can't do it for you. There's just one thing I can do for you. I can love you. When a pupil uses something a teacher gives, he's giving back.

JANE These past few weeks have been intense soul searching for me, with many long lost memories returning in my night work. Things I had totally forgotten or misinterpreted, I was now seeing with new eyes, and I didn't like what I saw. Qualities I had expressed but covered up or suppressed were surfacing to the extent that I sometimes didn't even recognize myself, and it was very hard to face. It filled me with remorse, shame, guilt. I didn't know, seeing that other side of myself revealed, how I could reconcile the person I thought I was with the person that was exposed. I felt terrible about myself.

And just at a point where I was feeling the greatest sense of worthlessness, I felt a pat on my back, I saw an etheric arm around my shoulder encouraging me, accepting me. I realized the cause of my despair and was instantly healed of that despair. You so often speak of the love that exists on the other side of life. I really felt that love in this experience. I needed that pat on the back!

******

PART III

SPIRITUAL CONNECTIONS

THE PLANES AND NIGHT TRAVEL TO HEAVEN

LIVING IN TWO WORLDS

Our physical existence on Earth and the invisible realms beyond us are intricately interconnected. Life and death are one coexistent reality. When this earthly life we're living draws to its end and we step into the next world into a new condition with new surroundings to inhabit other dimensions of reality, our consciousness goes with us to the extent that we have developed it on earth. Death is not extinction; there is a hereafter where we live on in the plane of Heaven we have earned.

The link between this life and the Afterlife becomes stronger and stronger as you progress in the Planes. The so-called `other world' is as close as our hands and feet. One way of accessing it is by visiting the heavenly planes in our sleep.

The planes of the etheric world of Heaven are populated by temples and halls of learning where, guided by heavenly teachers, we examine our lives and receive healing energy for growth and change. In each temple are examining rooms in which one's entire life is reviewed before the teachers. We see ourselves clearly through mirrors that reveal our entire self, the reality of ourselves as we truly are.

In these mirrors, we see the mistakes we've been making and how we can change our lives. Black mirrors reveal our detriments and in clear mirrors we see our positive attributes. We deal with memory patterns buried in the subconscious – guilt, fear, anger, criticism, resentment, selfishness – as we seek to overcome negative traits, make changes in our lives and reach the next level in our spiritual development. Earth states of consciousness are given healing.

Our night work experiences are often symbolic. The experiences we bring back from the temples go very deep into our subconscious, deeper than can be conveyed in words, and have a special individual meaning for the person who experiences the symbol. There are no earth words to describe in what way these night teachings impress us, the imprint they leave on our souls.

Before we came into our present lives, our souls dwelled in the heavenly realms on the plane we had earned. When we graduate from the life we are now living, our soul will gravitate to the plane we have gained in this round of our experience on Earth.

****

THE SILVER CORD

When we contact that other world every night in sleep, our spiritual bodies are connected to our physical bodies by the spiritual cord, also known as the silver cord. This cord, which is attenuated when traveling out of the body, is referred to in Scriptures (Ecclesiastes 12:6-7): "Or ever the silver cord be loosed ... then ... the spirit shall return unto God who gave it," and was known to exist from time immemorial. The silver cord remains attached throughout our nighttime experiences; it is not severed until the transition of death, as we call our graduation from this earth school.

As we travel out of our bodies, the spiritual part of us is lifted above material forces, while the physical body remains inert. In Mary Weddell's Color teaching, the silver cord that extends for night travel is named the "Sixth Ray of Yellow," which belongs to the "Spiritual Arc of Yellow," called "Illumination." The ray is described as "....pale silvery blue/white with a pale yellow underlay ... a living ray ... radiant, permanent, seen in all auras ... is the lifeline that guides the soul's return to the physical body in soul travel ... stretching as far as needed ... is severed only at death."

The silver cord is like an etheric counterpart of the physical umbilical cord. When attenuated when one is out of the body, it stretches as far as is needed for out of the body travel.

As Mary described it, "We have light bodies in the spiritual body. So as a glove is to the hand, so the physical body is to the mental and the spiritual body. When we go over permanently (after death) we take with us that mental body and the spiritual body.

"When we go as a band together at night, it reminds me very much of a cable car. We travel together in a line, one behind the other on etheric lodestones, hands on shoulders of the person in front of you. When you go over a lodestone, it's a lift and a lift and another lift. You feel that lodestone picking you up as you go on. It's a very steep ascent and quickly done. That vibration holds. We know we're in more power. The only way we can break the vibration is by speaking."

GRAND CENTRAL STATION

Starting at midnight, our class would spend some five hours each night in training on the Other Side.

First landing was on the 3rd Plane, where we stopped briefly for orientation at a gathering area that Mary euphemistically called "Grand Central Station." Many crowds of people are landing here, people from all over the world. Here one waits until being told where to go next, then our group would branch out to other heavenly locations for work in the temples at locations on the 4th Plane and higher.

As Mary's students, the class went to certain basic temples each night of the week, following which we would visit additional temples. The regular temples were: Monday night, the Temple of Wisdom; Tuesday night, Family Night; Wednesday, Temple of Bells; Thursday the Temple of Realization; Friday, the Temple of Harmony; Saturday, the Temple of Worship; Sunday, the Temple of Song, followed by family visits with our loved ones who dwell over there.

****

117

THE SLEEP WORLD

Sleep can be a very active state. During sleep, all people go somewhere, whether to the Planes of Heaven with a teacher, or they go to the Sleep World. A location spoken of in the Bible, the Sleep World is a rest area for souls who are not in spiritual work on the planes. In the Sleep World, the soul experiences dreams that are filtered to the intelligence of the dreamer, which in some instances will awaken the dreamer's wish to advance spiritually, to be taken out in his sleep by a heavenly guide.

It is not necessary to have an Earth teacher to receive spiritual training on the planes; everyone who so desires can, with the assistance of a heavenly guide, visit the planes in their sleep. For readers who lack a living teacher and wish to travel nightly to the temples of heaven, the spiritual body emits an azure blue light that attracts a heavenly teacher who will take that soul to the higher realms for learning.

AWARENESS OF TWO WORLDS

What is truly ours in the eternal realm? We have all of our memories; we have all that we have lived in this life within our mind. We know the people we've been with. We're aware of all that has been placed in the fullness of our lives. So as we are conscious living human beings on this Earth plane, when we go to the next world, we take with us and present just what we are, not what we think we are.

The purpose of all the planes is evolution of the Spirit. Within, you have a plan of your life that was etched upon your soul when you came into earth incarnation. On the Other Side, both in this life and in the Afterlife, you can pick up knowledge, re-form it, reschedule your life and make an adventure out of doing it.

When we're taken out by a teacher and arrive on a plane for development, our soul is intensely awake and entirely conscious upon that spiritual plane. We see, hear and sense the presence about us of those who are waiting to receive us. We understand why we're here. We know that before we can expect enhanced consciousness, we have to create desired chemical changes in the spiritual body, partake of a new atomic essence that entering the higher life requires. In our night work over there, we learn to live in these heavenly bodies for short periods of time. Each of us undergoes very personal experiences, soul memories which we bring back to our ordinary consciousness and incorporate in our lives.

GENE Do these memories come through exactly as dreams?

MARY Dreams, visions and hearing. We can say we dreamed, we heard of a voice saying thus and such. We haven't a language that will express what we're bringing through. We're short of words to explain it, because of the immensity of it. It's a world of universal teaching, and you come back with something that appeals to your own life. And another person may not receive that at all in the same temple. A person receives just what is their due.

TESTS

At night when our souls travel to the higher realms, we're given tests, following which we'll have a parallel test in the physical life. These tests are a means of unfolding consciousness. The higher the plane, the more difficult the test.

HANK   Could you say something about the different type of tests we have over there?

MARY The tests we're given on the spirals of each plane are designed to meet the need of the individual. Tests we face there and the ones we face here, we account for there. You're given fire, water and air tests: the fire tests deal with physical purification; water tests purify the emotional body; and the mental body is cleaned in air tests. There is specific testing and development in each temple, and afterwards, there will always be an earth test to match.

MIRIAM WILLIS   This may come to us in symbols and configurations revealing the dark side. There is specific testing and development in each temple, and our consciousness is given healing.

MIRIAM ALBPLANALP   I remember a recent fire test which brought this to mind, that the fire test cleanses and purifies the physical because the physical is the most gross of the three bodies; thus the water test, being next lightest in fluidic and wave length content, helps cleanse the mental /emotional body of our being; and the air test, being of the highest vibratory rate and lightest material, would cleanse and purify our spiritual body.

MARY   We call them water tests when we go through waters, and again many people have said to me, I know I went through that river, and when I came out, my clothing was dry.

MARGARET   I've been aware of a great many tests this week. I had a distinct feeling of shifting gears. Some things have been a lot harder and others have been a bit easier. I recall having a fire test.

MIRIAM WILLIS   We think of the wonder of fire, how fearful it is in its wrong place, how destructive not only to material things, but the fire of anger, the smoldering of remembrance, the thick smoke screen of escape mechanism. And we may think of the loveliness of fire--its warmth, its coziness, its light; the comfort it brings; the fellowship of uplift and joy; the purification.

When we think of it in our meditative thoughts, things come back that need to be burned away. We even have the experience of actually going through the fire of purification, burning away the dross and causing the gold of life to be molded in purity. And we think of the flame of spirit that never goes out, that is a lighted way within us, and how the breath of the Holy Spirit stands in a greater light and greater flame, greater usefulness and emanation.

Then, think of the fire of the sun, the great life giver. Without the sun of life, we would wither and die. And we think of water, how cooling it is, how refreshing, how terrible the floodgates of disaster, how wonderful the beauty of the ocean, the rivers and lakes, the living waters of life that refresh and renew us, that lift us, that purify our emotions; and how these two, fire and water, light and refreshment and vitality, balance themselves.

****

CLASS QUESTIONS AND EXPERIENCES

PATTI   What is the significance of a very rapid movement of the body while having a dream or vision?

MARY   I think that's going into that vibration where the soul itself almost resists. In this case, if this is a sensation that you bring back with you, then you too rapidly come back to your bed from your night work.

PATTI   This is sometimes quite prolonged, and it's like a movie that's been speeded up.

MARY   That's where we go over and come back. We're on a ray and we go very swiftly. What you're describing is the sensation that stays with you from that. Often you feel the entrance of the spiritual body or soul; you feel that you've risen or fallen a great distance.

MIRIAM WILLIS   Development helps balance that, so that you don't feel the rising and falling.

HANK   How long are we over on the other side each night?

MARY   We work over there about five hours a night. We're in the Sleep World the rest of the time. Three hours in the temples and two hours for general work.

MIRIAM WILLIS   You know, our work in the temples at night, though we don't always consciously bring back what we

121

experience, has nevertheless deep roots in the innermost being, and affects our whole life. Many times the reflected experience from the temples at night will manifest itself in a most surprising and practical test in the human life. Often the neophyte is looking for something spectacular, beautiful and wonderful, and when it doesn't come to us exactly like that, we just don't recognize that God is training us.

MARY We're given tremendous energy and enlightenment in the temples, but usually bring back just fragments – things to piece together bit by bit. For a considerable length of time, we may not be conscious that anything is happening. That's why this training requires faith that endures until finally the seeker proves by his own experience. It can be slow progress.

MIRIAM WILLIS "The vineyards are ripe but the workers are few."

MIRIAM ALBPLANALP Mary, speaking of the influences, isn't it true that the condition of consciousness in the soul affects the place it will find itself in, that if over there one suddenly becomes angry, they will automatically lower their vibrations and find themselves down?

MARY They just naturally go down. Let's say "the elevator" takes them right down, and they disappear for a time until they become poised again; then they can go back to where they were.

MIRIAM WILLIS And if you become critical over there, you suddenly find yourself isolated.

ALMA JOHNSON I wonder, Mary, if I could have unconsciously become conscious of the Magnetic Field. Not long ago, I woke up about 1:30 a.m., and I heard such pitiful crying just before I became wide awake.

MARY It was not the Magnetic Field. The Magnetic Field is vibratory activity that belongs to that netherworld where we don't go. When we go up through the Channel, we don't enter that nether land. The Channel protects you from seeing ugly faces and different points of Hades, and that's the reason for the Channel.

FRED   This is what the Tibetan Book of the Dead speaks of, the demons and ugly beings one encounters when unprotected. That's avoided when we go through the Channel.

MIRIAM WILLIS   We go up in Color, in the Channel, instead of being tormented and having fear of what we're going to see on the way up.

MARY   So you saw something else, Alma. Would it have been Wednesday night?

ALMA   Well, it was about a week ago. I'm not sure what night it was.

MARY   We've twice gone to hospitals where there were accident victims and a great deal of fear and suffering. As a group, we went on a quest of mercy, and you were with us, Alma, so that might have been reflective in your dream.

ROWENA   That was Wednesday night?

MARY   Yes. We have had four missions this week and two the previous week.

MARGARET   I wonder if some newer class members may not know that part of our training on the other side is that we sometimes go on missions to help in times of distress ... like to minister to earth victims of flood, fire and other disasters.

LOLA   Before we reach a plane that we're ready for, are we ever taken to upcoming planes to see where we'll go in our future night work?

MARY   You have previews and some lectures that prepare you for a change. Also, remember the chemistry in the spiritual body is waiting for us. We have to change. Realize the soul becomes enamored with its new vibration.

WILLARD   I know the temples have always been, but I wonder if they are all completed or are there some they're still working on.

MARY   Nothing that I know of, Willard; it would be high in the heavens beyond where I could ever go.

HANK   Do people who don't go to the planes for spiritual training also have dreams?

MARY   They do. Dreams come from either the Sleep World or from night work.

MARGARET   I know there's no formula, but are there any suggestions to help us in our night work?

MARY   Yes, the realization that you're going, that you have been and that you will go again. There's a time just before we sleep when we're very quiet. I have always likened that to the word "repose," that very quiet sensation. That's the time when the eyes are opened to the next world, you see things you haven't seen before, you're aware of them and face them in that cool of repose. Images may float there for quite some time, though sometimes you can't quite bring them through. You eventually will do so in pictures, in symbols, in visions.

******

COLOR

The basic foundation for the Planes group was Mary's unique and elegant "Creative Color Analysis" course, a study more far reaching than any other color teaching found in today's world. The Color teaching was an integral component of our Planes experience, complementing it beautifully.

The Color path is a mystical journey toward soul development. We live in a universe powerfully designed by color, whose energy is both visible and invisible. In Mary's classes and in those taught by Mary's senior teacher Miriam Willis, we explored color with emphasis on the etheric colors of the invisible world, which become visible when our higher senses are attuned, when we have developed spiritual sight and hearing.

In the invisible world are many octaves of light. Just as each color has its own individual wave length, so each has a message and a special effect. Color is the starting point of a journey toward inner purification. It's a never ending lifetime study, a joyful discipline that adds a pleasant, light touch to life. It's a gentle way to develop spiritually that eases the path and helps one's growth and ongoing. Using Color can create changes in people and conditions that bring them into balance.

Color is light revealed—vibration, energy, the visible essence of the life force. Color can be used to convey meaning between ourselves and the Creator; between the ego and the inner self, and to help and heal. Color bridges the physical and the higher dimensions. With color, we can dissolve negatives and create positives. Color establishes harmonious relationships.

Everyone is influenced by color, whether consciously or subliminally. Healing with color is an ancient art. According to records, the Egyptians, Essenes, Greeks, Buddhists, Hebrews, Persians and Tibetans all used color for therapeutic purposes. The study of Creative Color Analysis is a system of inspired and thoroughly tested spiritual development that Mary brought through from the Other Side.

MARY   Colors are spiritual food. Eat in color, drink in color; areas of the mind will open up that were not open before. Learn to work with the rhythm of Color. You will have one hour a day extra when you learn to live in Color. When you're tired, work in Color. Pour color on those at work. This is praying without ceasing.

Keep in clear, centered in spirit, where frustration can't touch you. Flood yourself with Color, for colors are the love and power of

God. Surround other persons absolutely with the royal purple color of faith, with the conviction that Color is going to work. Take the living form and see what you can do with lifting and loving it.

The story of Mary's discovery of color is relayed more thoroughly in the second book of the Planes series, *Everything You Always Wanted to Know About Heaven But Didn't Know Where to Ask.*

******

THE PSYCHOLOGICAL AND SPIRITUAL RAYS OF CREATIVE COLOR ANALYSIS

Color rays embodying both positive and negative qualities are used in development and healing. The more than one hundred fully tested color rays Mary brought through from an advanced state of consciousness from the Other Side consist of:

Four Psychological Arcs of twelve rays each, totaling 48 psychological color rays (Green, Red, Blue and Yellow); and Five basic Spiritual Arcs of Color with twelve rays each totaling 60 spiritual rays:

The Spiritual Arc of Green - Growth
The Spiritual Arc of Red - Metamorphosis
The Spiritual Arc of Blue - Training of the Ego
The Spiritual Arc of Yellow - Illumination
The Spiritual Arc of Purple - Spiritual Balance
Plus a number of what are called "Extended Rays"

Many, indeed most of these colors are not simply shades, hues or tints, but combinations of colors containing mid-rays, or colors described as either "streaked with", "tipped with," "touched with," "dirtied with," "overlaid with," "underlaid with," "with side shadings," "striated," "striped," or "swirling."

There is no quick way to describe Mary's elaborate and beautiful color teaching, for it surpasses any other "color system" available, as it is on a deeper, far more spiritual level. Mary's "Creative

Color Analysis" is a lifetime study, a matchless spiritual and practical aid toward development.

In Mary's own words: "Color and the Channel were given to me to challenge me and cause me to worship God more reverently. Color brought me serenity. The Channel brought me balance in thinking, patience in waiting for belief to develop into faith's unique security.

"Color helps the seeker to discipline his speech that he may seek clarity rather than cleverness, sincerity instead of sarcasm. The seeker knows that disciplined thinking and action give him wisdom and grace to accept life's pattern as traced upon his soul at birth. He realizes these patterns will be given him again through dreams, visions and the revelations received in his night work on higher Planes.

"If one becomes a seeker, he accepts the fact that his life is strictly between himself and God. The proof of man's development is private, personal, intimate, and spiritual beyond the compass of speech; too sacred, too vast, too fragile to be poured into the cold, unsympathetic molds of human language. Development of spiritual power through the Color Channel is an intuitive gift that causes one to burst forth in the rapture of faith and to listen for the whispers of love and promise of eternal life."

For those who wish to learn more, I recommend the book *Creative Color Analysis*, by Mary and some of her students; and you may wish to access http://www.creativecolor.org, in which many of Mary Weddell's revolutionary teachings on Color and other subjects are presented.

******

THE AURA

Etheric substance is that which is seen by many as the first level above the level of the material, an emanation surrounding and extending beyond the physical body. This is called the aura. The human aura is defined as the Kingdom of the Soul, and the Color path is a mystical journey toward the soul's development.

ESTHER BARNES   Mary, for the sake of the new people in the class, could you say something about the aura? Everyone is always interested in this subject.

MARY   The aura, the emanation surrounding and extending beyond the physical body, is under scientific scrutiny often called the energy field, which scientists have described as light radiating from the body in the form of photons. This energy field is a primary communicator between living species. We affect one another through our auras. When two auras are harmonious, the chemistry is there; inharmonious auras lead to discord. The major part of our auras are ever changing with the shifting circumstances and vicissitudes of life. When we lose control, such as in an anger flare up, the spiritual aura goes.

ESTHER BARNES   Some of us see partial auras, that is, we see some color, especially around the head of another person. We know that being able to read a full aura is very unusual, that is, seeing the many colors that extend for several feet around, above and even under the entire human being, being able to see and interpret the changes that go on continually around the entire body. I was wondering if you are always reading our auras, reading them continuously?

MARY   Only as the teachers come and your auras are revealed to me for your own growth do I take advantage of reading auras.

MIRIAM WILLIS   In Mary's color teachings, we study the 17 permanent rays of a Master's aura and their meanings, qualities we're looking to develop in ourselves. In our ongoing spiritual development, we endeavor to acquire desirable permanent rays such as these as we go along, and to be aware of the changes that happen in our non-permanent rays.

MARY   Reading auras is an art, perhaps—you can call it that. It's something that you acquire through the development and the chemical change of the human body. Many people have the gift, the art of doing it was given them, but they don't pursue the course.

******

KEYNOTE COLOR

Every person possesses their own keynote color and keynote of sound to which they vibrate, which act as their personal stimulation; each person projects his own aura of color vibrations emanating from within, flowing outward and following the contour of the body after the manner of a cocoon, or as some have said, an egg.

The keynote color is above the head, the topmost color in the aura, that which holds the keynote sound enwrapped.. As we develop, the spiritual aura widens and grows out. A flawless spiritual aura belongs to 20th Plane persons. Not before.

MARY If we can keep ourselves conscious of our keynote color, then we're intrinsically using it. We just naturally express it if we can get into the color itself.

WILLARD Do we usually wear our own keynote color in the temples?

MARY I believe in going to any temple, you'll be in your keynote color the moment you enter. When I'm taking you out, I'm asking you to be robed in the color of the royal purple of faith, and also, on the way over, I believe the rose purple of divine imagination is a wonderful color to put around you. It makes the going very easy, otherwise sometimes there's a tug, someone loses their balance and down they go; the vibration is broken, they'll arrive back on their bed with a bump and wake up. Then someone will tell me the strangest thing happened: I had an experience, I was sure I was going over but I found myself just bouncing on the bed.

****

THE CHANNEL

Color bridges the physical dimension with the higher dimensions. The Channel is our spiritual connection between the earth plane and higher states of consciousness. The highest spiritual colors, our birthright, are contained in the "Channel of Our Being," also called "the Keys to the Kingdom." This inner portion of a human being is the path of light leading his consciousness to higher realms of understanding.

There are twelve Keys to the Kingdom of the Soul, twelve spiritual colors being the inner portion of the human being, opening the way to illumination and intuitive perception.

We access the Channel through 4th dimensional consciousness in an uplifted state. We also commune directly with it by visiting the Planes of Heaven in our sleep. The Channel is our spiritual connection between the earth plane and higher states of consciousness.

MARY Imagine that there is this Channel of Color, that we want to enter it, and that entering that tunnel isn't any more than entering any other tunnel. We find that rotating in that tunnel is as a sleeve within a sleeve. The Color begins to revolve with the movement of this inner sleeve and to shed radiant light. Those are the stronger lights of the auric Channel. The Channel is really a vibrating stream of light that changes rapidly.

In our training as developing people, we go through the Channel of our being, the Color Channel, the "Keys to the Kingdom." The Channel is our spiritual connection between the earth plane and higher states of consciousness. When we're in the Channel we bypass the lower astral realms. While in the Channel one is never exposed to negative forces. We're protected. We can refine and balance our chakras, our mind and emotions, our spiritual being, with daily use of the Channel.

In development we're trying to change ourselves, to create a new chemical order of the body.

******

KEYNOTES

KATIE   I have a question about the keynote.

MARY   It was given you as a gift from the Father when you came into this world. What does your keynote do? It becomes a chord of music in your life. It vibrates through the entire being and becomes a chord of color music.

When you play the piano, and I know you do, look for your keynote on your fingers. After a little while, the flashing of that color comes to you and you'll realize the chord of your life is being played. It sometimes takes a lifetime to see this color in music, but color has been there all along. You know the song, "The Lost Chord" – those words are very revealing to me. I've always loved it. The composer, Sir Arthur Sullivan, and the woman who wrote the lyrics, Adelaide Anne Proctor, hoped that at the end of life, the rest of the chord would be given. That's the story of the lost chord. It's very true.

MARGARET   This was brought on by an intense desire to find out how one tunes in to the keynote. I kept wandering about it for weeks. This time I saw a musical instrument, a lute. I was given this: "All colors may be seen and heard. Let the colors flow and glow. Keep the strings tuned through your keynote. Anchor them well in the cup of life, which is the bowl of the lute, and know that this is but the touchstone, the memory spot of all the color that is.

"Everyone on Earth should have a memory aid to help keep in tune, something with a lovely sounding box for reverberation, a violin, lute, organ, a piano. The instrument is a heavenly tuning fork or gauge. Take it into your heart. In your absence from these heavenly halls, it is still attuned to your heart and soul. It grows and increases in tonal quality and range with each of your Earth victories of spirit, and creaks a bit at your slips when the colors fade. The lute is like the backbone."

****

DIVINE IMAGINATION

MARY There's a point where from the bridge of imagination we enter into divine imagination. The 4th ray of the Spiritual Arc of Purple, the color of divine imagination, is the open door to higher consciousness. One learns to distinguish between psychological imagery and spiritual imagery or divine imagination. Both are needed. Our ability to envision a possible occurrence, to hear inwardly, to close our eyes and journey in imagination, or to envision a stage drama while reading a play is a great gift. The color of divine imagination can assist one in developing and balancing whatever talent one has along this line.

MIRIAM The color of divine imagination - who can tell us?

MARGARET A rose purple, almost like a purple-amethyst.

MARY Fantasy and daydreaming are also forms of imagination. All of these lie in the realm of psychological imagery. This ability to create mental pictures is related to the ability to receive visual impressions from the higher realms, to have visions and to recall dreams. Persons who claim to have no ability to receive mental pictures may have blocked the ability or may be expecting too much—pictures clear as photographs, for instance. They may be skilled in some other form of communication such as directed writing.

Someone said, don't you have to combat the imagination? If a person so lives, imagination grows into divine imagination. The line of demarcation becomes so slight that they themselves might not know it. If you look at the aura, you would know that they've gone into divine imagination. They can go up that tower of delight and bring something back.

****

DEVELOPMENT

What is development? Development through Color eventually means the progression of spiritual talents, seeing with spiritual eyes, spiritual hearing, and the reading of auras. When one has opened his vision to the color scheme of the universe and his ears to the wonderful harmony around, he knows higher seeing and hearing bring with them added power, peace and usefulness. It's a part of higher consciousness to be able to see our aura and hear our chord.

VIOLET Some have likened development to the attainment of the gifts of the Holy Ghost: wisdom, understanding, counsel, knowledge, fortitude, piety, and "fear of the Lord," which is not the common definition of fear, but really means "wonder and awe."

ROWENA. I hardly ever see anything with my eyes open, but once in a while I do receive this little fleck of brilliant light. It happened recently; it was the first time in a long time. It was right there, right beside Mary, like a diamond. A glimpse of a diamond. If there's more you can tell me about it, wonderful. Otherwise I am happy.

MARY Usually development comes a great deal that way. Because you see light. But it doesn't stay with you,. Know that the next time it comes, if you have faith, it will be larger, longer, and it will meet you somewhere or it will give you a kind of message; it will be impressed upon your mind.

KATIE What would five beds all in a row, each with hands and each with a purple bedspread mean?

MARY It's a development of spiritual sensing. You should be able to work that out with your piano. Colors will be on your hand at the piano. That's where I would apply that, in your playing. You also paint. It's the sensing with the hands, and of course the purple is faith, isn't it? Sight and hearing come to us through development.

****

COLOR PRAYER

MARY   We're so used to talking. We have to learn to trust wordless Color prayer. On these planes we have many great prayer stations where our prayers, taken in color, can be activated. And these selfless prayers start to work there.

MARGARET   I wanted to ask about when we pray in color for other people. I find lately that if I'm facing east, say, and the person I'm thinking about is behind me, west, I feel uncomfortable!

MARY   Then I'll just say this, if you'll forgive me. In God's sight there is no east, west, north or south. So we have to take it from the channel of ourselves. We're just going up; we're just sending. See?

MARGARET   I was trying to feel the person more vividly. What, in prayer, are we supposed to do?

MARY   It's supposed to be a brief prayer in color. We're supposed to vibrate in this color long enough that after a short while you'll feel as if you've taken a long breath.

PATTI   If a group of people were sitting in prayer for someone for half an hour, they might use a plume only a couple of minutes of that time. Is that so?

MARY   That's true, and if you want to repeat it in fifteen minutes. I wouldn't do it any more closely together than that.

****

MORE CLASS EXPERIENCES

BARBARA   I was traveling in an unusual conveyance alone, up a high mountainside, wondering if I would make my destination to the top. I finally did make it, then wondered if I'd be able to park this conveyance. It was not exactly a car, but I think it was something that I built myself. I was able to park it easily.

The area was beautifully landscaped, and my destination was an area built into the side of this rocky place, high up the mountainside. A group of people, among them a number of my relatives on this side of life whom I haven't seen in a long time, were there. As we looked out into the vastness, a great sunset or sunrise glowed rose and golden in the ethereal blue sky, and the colors just seemed to fill the whole sky. We were all looking and exclaiming about them because they were so beautiful. The significant thing to me was that I woke from this experience much refreshed and with some heavy earth loads lifted from my soul.

MARY That also was one of the hard spots in going to the temple. You had things revealed to you. They were also things that have changed your conditions at home, and that's a very true thing.

HELEN MARSH   Our group was gathered in an ancient wild oak grove. The branches spread out, making almost a complete ceiling over us. As I looked at the leaves, each one turned into a little balloon. Each one was clear, like a crystal ball outlined in beautiful vibrating rainbow colors. One of the trees started to drip. The essence of spiritual energy from that tree was dripping onto us. We were supposed to absorb it and become saturated with it so that the vibrations of our beings would be elevated and strengthened to receive a downpour of light.

JEANNE   I've seen amazing purple geysers over there on several occasions and have mentioned them before. This past week, I remember seeing a whole series of these incredible purple geysers rushing up as I walked toward a temple.

Then, inside the temple, I was in a narrow corridor. It had a wall of gold bricks or bars with the bright color of the third ray of spiritual blue around it with a shield of gold, and there was a room at the end of a ramp. This color is interesting, because of helping to make one aware on different levels, both outer and within.

Outside, I also saw a pit that was like a mound with a very fine, flaky, substance that was soft like new fallen snow, made of all these beautiful spiritual colors of inspiration, the soft greyed rose of the 12th of spiritual red, meaning a universal concept of life; the pink color of aspiration, crimson-purple colors, and very pale lavenders and pinks.

HELEN VON GEHR A vision came to me in which I was on an upper level of a temple. There was an enormous bell. As I was wondering whether I was going to be able to go farther into the temple, a large hand formed, beckoning me. The hand was an outline, not solid, but outlined in what starlight would be. And the words were, "Not yet." While I was thinking about this, I saw a flower pot coming out of which were branches like in flower arrangements. And there were three golden fruits; there were leaves; and finally, behind that there was a sunflower. At the heart of the flower was a lovely face.

MARY Very, very promising.

HELEN MARSH In a vision or dream, I pulled a man from dirty water and helped him get clean.

MARY A source of high interest will prove something to you. Work it out; ask the guides.

RALPH   On Monday evening I saw a midnight blue background, then the shape of a lamp. The lower part of the lamp, which was actually a basket, looked like a burner on a stove. Petals the color of the cobalt color of the 4th ray of spiritual blue, meaning the control of emotion, were sticking out all around.

MARY That was a personal symbol of development. You've been carrying your light for a long time. I can look back a lot of years, about twenty years you've been carrying your light. The first inclination was to go the Buddhist way, because it seemed such a serene passage; and now you have moved into, shall I say, the Christ way, which is all the same Path.

Buddha loved his people enough that he gave up everything for them; Christ loved his people enough that he gave up his life for them. Now how do we know that Buddha did not give his life, too? I do not know that. I just know that Buddha came as a master, a great teacher of his people and gave teaching we can all benefit by. Then Christ came as a gift from God; he had many, many times come to different types of people and given his teaching. And while he was here, the number of years that he lived, he went to many nations and left his mark there.

RALPH Last Sunday I saw several pillars in the brilliant red lilac color of the holding force for the band of teachers. There was a blue background filled in, and the map of the northern part of the United States pulled up like a curtain.

PATTI I saw a white flower. It looked like a lilac but it was pure white with shading at the top. I heard beautiful words and I saw them written out, streaming along a line. It was something very inspiring about love. I wish I'd been awake so I could have written it down. I hope it will come back again.

MARY We usually see things in formation like that. It will come again and eventually it turns out to be a real vision.

LOLA I received something. At the end of a long hall I saw a casket, and in it was a corpse. It opened its eyes; then it raised its head and it got out of the coffin. I thought it meant that something in the past had been finished.

HELEN FLATWED In a vision, I had a sudden flash of insight. I was looking down upon a sea of roofs that were domes and minarets, all in gold. The buildings were vibrant white. There was a gold white light that vibrated over in the atmosphere around it, and circling up above, cherubim and seraphim were floating around and blowing on horns.

MARY A heavenly vision, all right. You have brought back something from your night work, a temple where you've been.

JOHN I've been wondering about what I saw. I saw all this fire. I thought it must be a fire test.

ESTHER BARNES I too believe I experienced a fire test. This morning when I woke up there was the picture of a waterfall, but it was of like a fire-fall. You look into this light and see it as the light within, a collective light.

LOLA A few nights ago I had a vision of an Egyptian guide, but I was only seeing one side, just like a half of a person. I think it was the right side. I was seeing it to my left. And why would I see a half? What would be the significance?

MARY That's all your spiritual eyes could be open to at that time. You were seeing someone advanced on the planes. And a half vision is about all you could get.

******

ONE WORLD WITHOUT END, AMEN

The transition into the next world is a natural process, a simple change in consciousness, like stepping from one room into one which is infinitely fuller and more beautiful.

MARGARET What can we do spiritually for a person who is passing?

MARY For a friend or relative who's passing, wrap the person in soft rose, the color of love. Color goes a long way in helping people who are about to pass over from this world to the next. Think from the medical point of view what would ease their pain, then ease the disposition, then leave with them faith, the color of royal purple. Also put in salmon pink, that something bright might seize their consciousness away from pain and opiates. Expect help, and give thanks for it when it's received.

EMILY How would we begin the color treatment for them?

MARY Say a prayer: "Father, grant me the privilege of helping so and so," naming the person. You can climb the Channel with them to give relief. Say thank you at the end.

PATTI   As we know, many of those who are about to pass are in pain. Could you give us a plume for pain?

MARY   For pain, I would start with the green base, then go into nile green, followed by a pale orange bridge, then shades of rose, rosy red, red lilac going into the blush orchid color of serenity, the light blue lavender color of peace, plus a blast of the royal purple of faith.

HELEN DE CANT   I've been wondering about what I saw. I was pulling this man through so much fire. I wasn't sure who he was, but I cared deeply about saving him.

MARY   You can ask and you'll be told who the man is. It does make a difference to you in your vision or dream. You may have actually helped this person on the other side. It sounds to me like someone who has passed over and was not conscious of having gone over. You in some way were enabling him to become conscious of his passing, he became cleansed and knew his way. Anyway, it's something you're getting credit for, because the light is still around you. The point is, we can help someone who has passed over, or is passing.

MARGARET   Is it possible we may have helped someone in this manner without realizing it?

MARY   Many of us have helped someone in this way. Sometimes we don't understand how much we've done so. It's our recognition that's lacking. Or sometimes we have an inkling but we don't quite believe it.

ANDREW   This begs the question of spiritual sight and spiritual hearing, which is a goal we would all like to achieve. How possible might that be for people in this class?

MARY   There have been 4200 of my students that Miriam knows of who have been counted by the Brotherhood, 4200 people who have received sight and hearing. It's certainly possible for everyone who reaches for it, for all of you who use Color.

ESTHER ESTABROOK I sometimes feel I'm so far from that. I use color, I pray with color, I have faith, but my progress has been so slow. I wish I could bring back more from my night work.

MARY   Never be discouraged, Esther. Many of those people mentioned came to lectures and sat in classes for quite some time. And as they evolved, they came into that state of spiritual seeing or hearing. It just took time. So don't despair of bringing things back. They come in different ways.

Sometimes an experience will come back in such a practical fulfillment of some earth occurrence that we scarcely recognize it. And then it perhaps begins by a haunting something in our mind that causes us to wonder whether "that's linked with something I learned over there," because we sense in it, perhaps, a broader platform of understanding or wider area of forgiveness or love, or something that causes us to say, I believe I'm growing a bit. So these are things that are helpful to watch for.

WILLARD   Is there a pattern where you could trace their progress? Any similar signs?

MARY I noticed all the way through that the spiritual voice they heard was someone they respected or loved. And also, the face they saw was an intimate face. Today as I was thinking of all you dear ones, I thought how many of us have grown up with the idea that our loved ones are happier over there in heaven, so we shouldn't try to bring them back; that's what we were raised to think, isn't it? Why hold onto something that has gone into a different realm? But then, many people have heard the voice or seen a forgotten face.

One woman drew a picture, showed it to her mother, and asked her mother who looks like this? She didn't draw well, but she got the form of the face reflected in the mother's mind immediately. The mother identified the face. The daughter asked, "You mean that's Dad's grandmother? I've been seeing her over and over again."

Another woman had been in the hospital recovering from an accident. On a certain place on the wall as the morning light came in, she saw something. She asked one of the nurses, "Do you see anything there, over on that wall?" And the nurse said, "I see the outline of a woman with a shawl over her head."

EMILY If we sense that somebody from spirit is with us in the room, what should we do? How should we treat them?

MARY If I sense that someone is with me, I thank them for coming. Then if they still stand there, I ask what can I do for you? I would treat them just as if they were friends coming to my door.

EMILY I can't see them, I can't hear them, I just know they're there. I feel I should stand up, but I'm afraid to budge an inch. Should I stand up anyway?

MARY Certainly. Do stand up and greet them. You'd soon be poised, back in balance. If the spirit moves swiftly, sometimes we're taken short. One woman said to me, "I've prayed for ten years that my father would come to me! The other night I walked into a room and there was my father. What did I do? I screamed my head off. My husband was alarmed and asked what was the matter. He thought I was ill. I just hated to think I was such a coward when my own father came. Had I only pretended I wanted it?"

I told her no, it's the rate of vibration. Your father has been over there about thirty years, and the rate of vibration, coming into the room unexpectedly, is what caused her fear. Now if she'd been writing back and forth to her father over the years, it would lift imagination, with the infinite love that would have been between them, he would have come in on that ray and she would have sensed him without fear. If you sense it before you see it, that's all that's necessary. So awareness is one of our key words.

JEANNE I had a vision upon waking, but it was more than just a vision; I actually saw two spiritual beings with my physical eyes. These forms, encased in incredible light, were so clearly etheric energy from a higher realm. There was no mistaking it! The two figures were dressed in colors of rose and green, like the 5th ray of spiritual green, the vibrant, vivid shade of green with the old rose midray. I found this interesting, since this ray awakens one into the understanding of higher universal forces.

In the past, I've been aware of loved ones visiting from the Other Side, but this is the first time I ever actually saw human forms with my physical eyes. It was so intense, yet so quick and evanescent that I wanted to hold onto it, capture it forever, keep it with me always. I'm grateful for having seen what I did, for this fleeting vision is so much more than I was ever given before. It was so real. But it was just a glimpse and it was gone in an instant.

MARY The length of the vision is the length of the chemical reaction. If in your everyday life you can get this, really hug it to you, it will help keep you among the balanced forces.

VIRGINIA I was wondering why I've seen my father so clearly this past week. He was ill before he passed.

MARY It's natural to hear or see a loved one shortly after he has gone over.

GENE I wonder how many people who've never thought about the Afterlife have second thoughts, almost maybe a conversion, as they lie dying.

MARY Few people at the end of their life, but who are sad if they don't accept a future life. All of us here know there is life after death; you wouldn't be here if you didn't. Until they meet up with a great need, most people think very little about it, unless development takes hold that we almost feel at a loss if we can't express it.

We face on the other side of life, just what we are here. All of you, at the setting of life's sun, will find the things you've left undone, the hard things to face, rather than those things we have willfully walked away from. As a group of people sitting here tonight, God himself would say they carried their burdens as best they knew how. The things we leave undone, the things we really haven't time for, many times follow us. Maybe we were supposed to see just one more thing that we didn't take time to see.

Now we speak of the temples where we've been to try to become less self-centered and selfless to the degree that man can live and work in this world and still find harmony and happiness. At the same time he must live with his fellow man, and we all know it's a small degree, perhaps, that we can perfect these lives of ours, especially when you're in the everyday world. We're trying to form a pattern by which we've lived at night in the temples. We're trying to bring back something to prompt your memory. Sometimes reviewing brings points forward, and these are the things that make you know you were there.

We're trying to gain the balance of our soul's worth and know the visions that come are given to us for our benefit. Many times in sharing, another will have had the same thing on the way up this ladder of development. I often find that two people not even knowing each other will be given something in the same temple, and it works out beautifully because they see that as a proof.

If we can go back to the thought that what we have, our hands are overflowing, really, if it's given through development. We have all we need and more. So we can always take time to share.

VIOLET   Mary, don't you think it's always true that when you've given something you feel as if you'd received a gift?

******

THE BOOK OF LIFE, THE HALL OF RECORDS

MARY   Some of us don't know why we're led to live with people who are an annoyance and a hardship. But in the end, when you're able to read the records over there, you'll know.

MIRIAM ALBPLANALP   Where and how do we find out about the reasons for that?

MARY The Book of Life in the Hall of Records. You can go back and see your life from the time you were sent into the world. One's future is written there also. Every plane contains records. This is one of the advantages of our night work: the teachers will take you to the Hall of Records. When we go further along in the planes, that explains itself better.

Test yourself when you're not in harmony with a parent, a child, a spouse, a friend, and see what it is in you. Because you're trying to overcome in yourself what you dislike in them. You wouldn't see it if it wasn't for that. You chose your father and your mother, whether you like it or not. And you chose a name, and when you came into this world, you didn't like your name and you got rid of it, your name is on the Book over there.

Our subconscious is that dark cave that has to be cleared of everything until the self revealing of the self becomes an open book to us. And God has made such a far reaching and marvelous provision for this that is within us, a provision that registers elsewhere as well. It registers in eternity in the Lamb's Book of Life. It registers, if you want to use another term, in the Akashic records.

MIRIAM WILLIS There are places in the heavenly world where these Akashic records are kept, everyone's. You know when Jesus said that the Father cares for the sparrows, and there's not a hair of your head that isn't numbered – this is truer than we think.

MARY Everything that has affected the life deeply is registered there. Even though we've tried both here and in our night work to clear our subconscious, if we've earned the right and the time is right for us to be taken to it, we're taken to the first Hall of Records, where we view past lives and the aggregate of the benefits and results of the failures and weaknesses throughout our many lives.

This is a an amazingly revealing thing. Now over and above being allowed to look into the record of life, when we're developed enough, we're allowed to see that Book, where we see exactly what God's purpose for us was in this life. It takes a degree of spiritual power to bring this back into the conscious mind.

GENE   How do we bring these things back? Through what mechanism?

MARY   The power is furnished through the growing, unfolding faculty of divine imagination. One thing that's very helpful is to draw that ray, the ray of divine imagination to us in order to spark our imagination. When we see that Book of Life, we know there's nothing lost in that land where the great Creator has made everything perfect.

HANK   How about after we've passed on? What kind of arrangements can be made to see the Book of Life then?

MARY   You will still want to go into the Hall of Records. You turn to see a lighted ray and follow it. You go to where the teacher is. And they tell you at a certain time, the following day...

ANDREW But if there's no time on the Other Side, how can you tell when they mean?

MARY   We say it's time as we have here, but there certainly is a rhythm of day and night, lessons, learning, lifting the soul. You can keep very busy over there. There's also a time when you rest. There's a great deal of meditation on the other side of life, because you have a lot to meditate upon. Your selfishness here has to be corrected there. As for time, they might say "after the Temple of Wisdom tomorrow."

And then, you go to the Hall of Records. The first thing you see is the record of your life. This present life is the important life. This is the thing you're enlightened upon almost immediately. And you go up there and you see yourself. If you've written a book, the book is there. If it was worth writing it will be in your hands, and you'll see certain sections that have been written out because it wasn't truth; it was a delusion. Sympathetic understanding is one of the laws of spiritual attainment. And that means that we've lifted ourselves on wings of enlightenment and that is on that record there.

You read what you've done in this earth life. After you've been there a good while and proven yourself, you're allowed to know your past lives. The Akashic Records are open to you after you have attained the 4th Plane over there, the Akashic Records, where you can read the records of your past lives.

MIRIAM WILLIS   Sometimes we're given experiences of jealousy and misunderstanding just that we are to have our eyes open, that we may grow in stature when it comes to correcting things when they're in the lives of other people whom we see are walking too close to the edge of the abyss of misunderstanding. One can get over that edge so quickly!

MARY These things are registered in the subconscious according to the depth of impression. Great shocks, traumatic occurrences, behavior patterns, poor health patterns, fears, depressions are registered in the subconscious.

ANDREW   Has this anything to do with divine imagination?

MARY It has a great deal to do with it, because those images rise up to confront us with the potential to overcome. Divine imagination is beyond our conscious mental imagination. It's linked to Christ Consciousness and the development of our soul. Everything that has deeply affected our life is registered in those records. The purpose of the records is simply that we may later, even though we have tried here to clear our subconscious, be able to see our record.

MIRIAM ALBPLANALP   There's something I remember about the library in the Hall of Records, a two-story library, with a kind of 1890-ish antique-y essence, as I recall, with heavy, regal, legal looking books, solid, substantial, musty-dusty. That must have been a little place where I was about to inquire about something related to the records.

MARY   We do know, Miriam, that on the other side of life, every book that has been written is there. Some of them are empty; they have nothing to read. And some of them have pages marked, they're so important to life. So everything is registered that has been done.

One man told me after he got over – he had been vindictive and very hard on the Catholic Church. He was a fine orator. This was a good many years ago. And when he went over he thought if there was any way to get back and change people's minds about Catholicism, that was what he was going to do. He had written so many books. He called someone whom he very much respected; he thought he would go to the Records so he could look up his own books. He had been told his books were there.

He went there and looked at them. The books were bound beautifully but they were perfectly empty. It was a terrible shock. He was not friendly to the teachers who offered to talk with him, so he retired to himself and stayed alone for quite some time. Then, as he told it to me, he said, "Something in their philosophy took hold of me, and I knew that I had ruined my life, the life of my friends and family from the pictures that they showed me of my earth life."

He was a great philanthropist, he gave the children's hospital in Schenectady, New York, and he was so very strong in his opinions. They tried to run him for a Senate seat one time, but he was so argumentative they knew he would never get elected.

There were many things that should have been pointers on his way, but he didn't pick them up. He never made that turn until he got to the other side of life. And then, because he knew me very well, he wrote this back to me, and, oh--a number of years later, he appeared in one of the classes. He'd had every chance in the world to have all the classes he needed, all the churches he needed. He was an Episcopalian, a dignified Episcopalian who spent his time talking against the Catholic Church.

That gives you a chance to know what I'm trying to tell you. So there must be dusty books that have been there a long time. You also see pictures that are beautifully framed, hung on the wall but are an empty canvas. This particular story comes very clearly to me. A man had painted a picture and it was not good. His friend had painted a better picture. His friend passed, and the man still living made an exchange, took his friend's picture, changed the name and took credit for it.

When he got over there, this subterfuge was on his conscience always. Before he passed, he had repented. But he wondered what he could do to make amends. He couldn't possibly admit it, you know. Well, somehow it catches up with us on the other side. And so, when he went to see this picture, it was just a canvas. There wasn't any paint whatsoever upon it. Hanging there was the beautiful frame that he had put it in. And then, as he was gazing at the blank canvas, the friend whose name he had taken off of the painting was standing right beside him, and the image came back when that man who had really painted it appeared.

The picture came back, they viewed it together, and the friend said, "It's all right with me; I don't mind at all." You see, we never get it entirely alone.

DALE Could you say something further about the Akashic Records and the definition of Akasha?

MARY Akasha is known as the all-pervasive life principle of the universe, a medium in which everything is contained. It fills all space and interpenetrates all matter. Indian philosophy interprets Akasha as ether, the subtlest element that permeates the universe.

Buddhists say Akasha is space bounded by the material world, an infinite, indefinable space that contains the material world. Historical records of all events and experiences, of all thoughts and actions that have ever taken place, are taking place now and will take place in the future are indelibly imprinted upon Akasha.

JOHN Why do we have these temple experiences so many times?

MARY The whole of our subconscious has to be cleared from the dregs in the well of being in the past, all we've seen or done or been influenced by has to be purified. We have to go down into the depths of our being to where lies the residue of the periphery of our lives, our relationships, and the world. We are all receptacles. So on the path, avoid negativity. It's not good to allow eyes and ears to take in violent things; it interferes with optimism and prayer power.

GLENN DIES If one does have dark dreams and visions, what should they do?

MARY When they come, envelop yourself in the power of the risen Christ, enter his presence and in that light read your dark picture. Speak of faith and be in his presence: "For lo, I am with you till the end of the world. " Be cruelly honest with yourself if you sincerely want to grow, don't make excuses or blame environment, relationships or anyone but yourself.

******

LIONS ALONG THE WAY

Mary often spoke of stumbling blocks on the path of development which she called the "lions on the path" or "lions along the way." It was part of our work to confront those lions and to subdue them. This was done both through Color, by "breaking old molds," facilitated through our nightly visits to the Planes, and by our following the Buddhist Eight Fold Path, which we began encountering on the Plateau between the 7th and 8th Planes, and more fully on the 8th Plane (to be covered in the next book of the Planes series).

Suppressed negative patterns stagnate development. Class

members confronted lions one by one, lions of anger, pride, deceit, greed, criticism, stubbornness, deviousness, hatred, selfishness, laziness, lying, cheating, dishonesty, envy, jealousy, ignorance, delusion, malice, slander, avarice, holding a grudge, aversion, fear, arrogance, negligence, denial, false concepts, criticism, deception, irritability, impatience, fear, doubt, resentment ... the list is extensive.

Lions can be tricky to scout out. Some hide from our awareness; some appear in unexpected ways. Some one might even consider to be virtues, but are actually traps in disguise. Some are subtle and hard to recognize, others we allow ourselves the latitude to indulge in, believing we have no choice, because we are, as they say, between a rock and a hard place, forced to act with no alternative, lest we be unable to continue the lifestyle to which we're accustomed. Sometimes we're even proud of our lions and wear them as a badge of honor. With the lions, our reactions are really put through the microscope. When we die, we leave with our habits, flaws, and unresolved business. This is one of the reasons "breaking old molds" is part of Mary's teaching.

We need to take charge of our emotions in order to change. Self-control over actions, mind over matter, control over mind and thought, the purification of intellect, heart, spirit, innermost consciousness and the deeply hidden must all be exposed to the light. We all learned much as we examined ourselves in the temples of the Other Side.

When you're given the list of lions and you start testing yourself, you're cleaning house for the next life. There are little hidden things in us that ought to be recognized and cleared out. They crop up again and again. We have the law of karma to contend with. Every action has its reaction, its karmic results. As ye sow, so shall ye reap – the law of cause and effect, the law of compensation.

We don't know how fear, pride, and anger are changed into faith, love, wisdom, and peace any more than we know how the soil changes a seed into the plant. It is inwardly silent and hidden, and we only know of it by comparison of successive states. As our heavier colors are transmuted into the Channel rays, we live in a state of not just closing our eyes and believing. We know.

The lion was the insignia of old Egypt. Jesus used all the ancient symbols, adding a greater degree of revelation of God's love and brotherhood of man, breaking through thick karma with redemptive love.

People are afraid to break through the shell of their set ideas, but when we've touched the vastness beyond us, we're more ready to receive truth. We have a bulwark of strength, we're not afraid to explore and discover hidden things, as we have the tethering that takes away fear. As we grow in this pattern, we climb the heights and we plumb the depths. God is infinitude. We receive revelations of the depths needing to be cleared as we're ready. Walking the path, you've seen and known that beautiful things, sometimes formed, sometimes formless, come through inspiration and the new insights flowing through us.

But sometimes as we go farther, the beauty slips away and dark side is shown. On the Eightfold Path, we recognize the lions so that the ego can be tempered from lion to lamb.

At the top of the Plateau we're told what we've done and left undone. On the way down we're told what the Eightfold Path holds for us. We're waiting to be called to that Eightfold Path. No teacher can do for you what needs to be done. God himself can't do it for you. You yourself have to overcome. No love of another can take away what God has given you to overcome. But there are many ways you can receive help for dispositional traits and for being reminded of these traits.

PATTI I didn't have an image or a vision for this, but I seemed to hear something, and it was about being nailed to the cross. I couldn't get the entire thing and I didn't know what it meant, but it impressed me very much and I couldn't get this phrase nailed to the cross out of my head. It seemed to be something that had been given to me in my night work.

MICHAEL If I may say something about being nailed to the cross ... I think this has to do with a lecture we heard about the Eightfold Path. Because in Buddhism, the first noble truth is that life is suffering, which is similar to being nailed to the cross. Being nailed to a cross is a metaphor for suffering. And the solution is following the Eightfold Path.

MARY Most of us, developed or not, have a cross to bear; we many times have been nailed to a cross. We could scarcely bear it, life has been so disappointing. The Book of Life records that. It's part of our purification on the Eightfold Path.

****

ARRIVING IN HEAVEN FOLLOWING DEATH

What happens after death? What awaits us when we leave this world? Life and death are one coexistent reality. There is a hereafter where we live on in the many planes of Heaven. As Jesus said, "For in my Father's house are many mansions."

When the silver cord is severed in "death," and we leave this world, crossing over to the other side to inhabit another dimension of reality, our consciousness goes along with us to the extent that we have developed it here on Earth. Every soul arrives via the River of Life at the Landing Field on the First Plateau of Heaven. It's an entrance filled with awe into that world. Immediately, you see surroundings of amazing beauty and intensity.

The newly deceased is met by loved ones who are waiting to greet him. The Hierarchy directs him to Restland for a period of seven days (and sometimes more), for rest, adjustment and preparation. Following this he goes to an area called Segregation, a place of revealing self to self, which poses testings and reflections from the life just lived, which leads him next to the area of Registration. Registration involves the Mirror of Life and passing seven tests before he can advance. Here is contained the life record he has established.

On then to the Examining Field, fourteen tests followed by healing centers of consciousness where body, mind and soul are healed. Next, Healing Areas and Healing Centers of Consciousness administer to the ills of body, mind and soul. Placing our own limits on ourselves, we are judged by ourselves.

For a more complete description of what takes place during the transition of death, you may wish to read the first and second books of the Planes series. They are: *Planes of the Heavenworld* and *Everything You Always Wanted to Know About Heaven But Didn't Know Where to Ask*.

****

SUBJECTS THAT APPEARED IN THE FIRST FOUR PLANES OF HEAVEN BOOKS

A host of metaphysical topics were raised in the four books in the Planes series. To mention just a few among many:

What happens after death? What can I expect in the Afterlife? Clearing the subconscious to advance spiritually; Night work, dreams, visions, tests; Communication between Heaven and Earth; Visiting departed loved ones on the Other Side; Heavenly helpers; angels, invisible guides and hierarchies; The Animal Kingdom; Babyland and Children's Land; The Suicide Plane; the Netherworld: Purgatory, Hell, the Magnetic Field; Earthbound souls; Prayer, healing, meditation; Music and art in Heaven; Developing spiritual sight and hearing; How Mary received enlightened knowledge of the Planes of Heaven; and much more.

****

MEDITATION CLIMBING THE CHANNEL
LED BY MIRIAM WILLIS

MIRIAM WILLIS Let us free ourselves of consciousness of the body. Let us clothe ourselves in our spiritual garment of the keynote color. Wrap the cloak of faith about you and see its beautiful royal purple color. This brings to our consciousness quite a settled feeling. It's foundationally good to feel settled, an absence of restlessness, a quietude and a peace that falls like a benediction on the soul. It's also the posture of waiting.

And there are so many attitudes that we experience in waiting. We wait sometimes in impatience, in irritation, in agitation. When we can transform that period of waiting into something peaceful and still, it just naturally turns to the outreach of prayer. We forget the lapse of time, for we're waiting enveloped in the Lord. We're waiting in the rhythm of the law. And to do this in moments from day to day as we need to is a wonderful practice.

It seems to bring an endowment to our being that causes us to live naturally in that rhythm of God's universe that develops within us a strength to keep the raucous tones of the pressure of the outside rush, the hustle and bustle, truly outside to such an extent that with practice we don't notice them as much. And this is good. These are the quiet moments that build strength into our being, that create the steady flame of a steady light.

This is the turning of the conscious mind to the greater outreach of that in which we live at all times, so that the life force begins to send out its ray of light throughout our being.

And now, let us see ourselves glowing with an infilling power of light that is centralized within, and as it glows and grows stronger, it radiates outward throughout our whole being. Now as we rest in that power, there is a renewing of strength as we just naturally mount higher. The weariness drops away. Let us often take that flight as though we rode on the back of the eagle in its flight, so strong are the everlasting arms beneath us.

We're resting, yet we're alert, listening and looking in expectation. It's good to stretch the faculties of the soul into the spiritual senses in this expectation. Let's practice it often and receive the surprise, if you will, of more abundant fruit.

And now, with our hearts full of thankfulness for the beauty of Color, for the power of those color rays, and the wonderful things they can transform in us, here in the stillness of this moment, let us climb the Channel together. Let us proceed upward, and either audibly or silently name each color to ourselves. Let us draw these colors to ourselves for a few seconds at a time. Each color gives a greater uplift and support to the spiral above it. Because each succeeding color is of a higher vibration than the one below it, we "climb" in consciousness while ascending the Channel.

We stand in the royal purple of faith and mount to the gray lavender of the holding force of patience, the delicate pink lavender of inspiration, the rose lavender of the spiritual voice and the blue orchid of prophecy, over the yellow bridge of enlightenment to the rose orchid of the message bearer, the red lilac of the holding force for the band of teachers, over the bridge of yellow enlightenment to the glowing peach of union of mind and spirit, the light blue orchid of brotherhood, the blush orchid of serenity, over the bridge of lightest green in desirelessness to the rose bisque of grace and the light blue lavender of peace.

And now we come to the effulgent Fount of Supply, where a door to the world beyond has opened. The union of our two worlds is realized, as we are seeing with the spiritual eye clearly into the higher planes at this gateway between the visible and invisible worlds. We have risen in 4th dimensional consciousness, where we are aware of the oneness of our two worlds. We know we are living in eternity now. Rest in the quietude of your lifted spirit in silent expectation. This is a time of communion with the Infinite.

******

155

THOUGHTS FROM MARY

Faith is a belief in the boundless. It is to breathe the air of the eternal. Faith is the tool with which man builds the Kingdom of Heaven on earth, creates a paradise out of pulverized dust. Laughter is the sunlight of the spirit. It lightens the burden of the so-called woebegone existence of man on the one hand, and lights up the sorrow darkened spirit on the other. Love's rose grows on the cross. It is pain as well as perfume. Tears are, indeed, a divine gift. They are a talisman for learning the secrets of the self. The silence of the spirit is the spirit of silence. Silence is the best of prayers. It is a vision and a whisper of the Eternal, the Infinite God. Bless you, Mary.

******

Let the Spirit of Christ reign in our hearts tonight. Let's see what we can bring forth for tomorrow's needs. Be it joy, may we share it. Be it sorrow, may we know how to overcome it. And may we use Color to overcome it, testing the law of give and take, the vibratory activity of Color in the life of the human being who accepts it and uses it as God paints the sunset. Just so, use Color in your speech, use it in your song, use it in outgoing love or any deep emotion that you feel. If it's an ill emotion, one that you do not wish to keep, wash it out with beauty.

We must, if we live in this world and make progress, take hold of the things that drag us down. Those things that are heavy that we carry, the weight of it that takes away the adventure of life, takes away the pleasant picture that naturally comes to us as we follow on the way. Let us be lifted up, lifting ourselves by our bootstraps.

As long as man has lived he has been told: beyond him lies a path, a path of enlightenment and unfoldment, and nothing is denied him if he can believe. And man does get a glimpse of it, and he does believe for a time. But it's hard to fasten your attention and keep it on an ambition for any length of time, unless it be a worldly ambition. If the Path becomes one with you, it is easily yours. But sometimes, something that we can't see with the physical eye is very difficult to keep centered on.

Oh dear Father, I open up to thee that thou mayest fill me with thy divine order that, refreshed, I may again pick up my load, be it hard or easy. Thy beloved son will be my true companion and thy whole spirit my guide, so I shall go ever forward and upward to thee. Amen.

******

I greet each one of you gladly and with love. I think there should be in our hearts a wealth of understanding of the peace where our brother stands today. We do desire peace. Within our very souls we long for peace. Is this not the time of a wider and nobler understanding?

Whether we believe that in the life to come, it will be as today or finer and more refined atmospheres to live in, are we willing and ready to accept all the tests that are before us? Can we say to the Father I will go where you want me to go?

That's a test, because the will of man operates with his ego and his ego overtakes him many times. It outshines, walks before him, leading him to paths of consciousness that are not true. I do believe that God intends us to develop our understanding. I do not think that it should be pinched and small because some teacher said "thou shalt not." I believe that man's will was given him to express, and that no one should control his will but he.

Man many times is bent and bowed under a load of fear. Therefore, his life is not what he wants it to be. Lift your load yourself. Stand enveloped in the power of universality and see what it will do for you. Within you is the knowledge, wisdom, and understanding. It's the self improvement that we're looking for in development, the happiness that comes from having evolved out of a basic pattern that you have set your way.

If the Path is entirely too familiar, take a detour for a time. Many times, we're shocked how negative we've become. And maybe we had no consciousness of becoming negative until the other person gives us the negativity of their thoughts. And we fall right into line. If I continue in this vein, the negativity will touch the development that is about me. I can't afford to do it. So selfishness along that line sometimes pays. I feel you have had the most trying times. I have been familiar with the many things that come into your lives, that have crossed your way, and you have withstood the hardships of being tested.

I will say this, that any shrewd group that can test themselves and use Color against the condition have proven a faith of development that cannot be proven any other way. And I thank God for Color that is such a healing force. Thank God for the devoted ones who in every phase of life, are doing God's work. Pity the person who doesn't want to do it, for they are desolate within themselves; they have not what you have.

Father in heaven, we do thank thee that we have come once again together in thy name, and thou hast said, where few are gathered in his name, there he is in the midst. And for the help that has been sent us, for each thing that has blessed our lives, and as the dawn comes tomorrow, may we remember that thou hast been near. And as at noontime, a thought of thee enter in, that Peace may come to the world. And when the sun has set, oh God, may we lay our head on the pillow knowing that the day has gone by and it is in thy hands. Bless thou our world. May we bless each other by the love we bear, each one. May every one of us realize the great truth that we live in Eternity now. In the Name of Christ our Lord, we thank thee once again. Amen.

######

.
.

.

ABOUT THE AUTHOR

Jeanne Rejaunier graduated from Vassar College, and did postgraduate studies in Paris, Florence, Rome, and at UCLA. While a student at Vassar, she began a career as a professional model, and subsequently became an actress in Manhattan, Hollywood and Europe, appearing on and off Broadway, in films and television, on magazine covers internationally and as the principal in dozens of network television commercials.

Rejaunier achieved international success with the publication of her first novel, *The Beauty T*rap, which sold over one million copies and became Simon and Schuster's fourth best seller of the year, the film rights to which were purchased outright by Avco-Embassy. Rejaunier has publicized her books in national and international tours on three continents in five languages. Her writing has been extolled in feature stories in Life, Playboy, Mademoiselle, Seventeen, BusinessWeek, Fashion Weekly, Women's Wear, W, McCalls, American Homemaker, Parade, Let's Live, Marie-Claire, Epoca, Tempo, Sogno, Cine-Tipo, Stern, Hola, The New York Times, The Los Angeles Times, The Washington Post, and countless other publications.

Rejaunier has written several other books, which are listed on the page "Other Books by Jeanne Rejaunier."

Branching out as a filmmaker, Rejaunier produced, directed, filmed, and edited the four hour documentary, *The Spirit of '56: Meetings with Remarkable Women.*

######

OTHER BOOKS BY JEANNE REJAUNIER

The Beauty Trap
The Motion and the Act
Affair in Rome
Mob Sisters
Odalisque at the Spa
Hollywood Sauna Confidential
My Sundays with Henry Miller
Titans of the Muses (with Noreen Nash)
Planes of the Heavenworld
Everything You Always Wanted to Know About Heaven But Didn't Know Where to Ask
The Kingdom of Heaven and 4th Dimensional Consciousness
The Afterlife in the Here and Now
Modeling From the Ground Up
The 50 Best Careers in Modeling
Runway to Success
Astrology For Lovers (with Lu Ann Horstman)
Astrology and Your Sex Life (with Maria Graciette)
The Paris Diet (with Noreen Nash and Monique de Warren)
The Complete Idiot's Guide to Food Allergy (with Lee Freund, M.D.)
The Complete Idiot's Guide to Migraines and Other Headaches (with Dennis Fox, M.D.)
Japan's Hidden Face (with Toshio Abe)
The Video Jungle (written under nom de plume)

#######

THE BEAUTY TRAP, by JEANNE REJAUNIER

"Here is a novel that can't miss, crammed with all the ingredients that make a blockbuster." - **Publishers Weekly**

"A startling closeup of the world's most glamorous business, an intensely human story." - **The New York Times**

"Jeanne Rejaunier has concocted a sexpourri of life among the mannequins that's spiked with all the ingredients of a blockbuster bestseller."- **Playboy**

"A fascinating inside story of the most glamorous girls in the business, absorbing to read." - **California Stylist**

"A powerful novel that takes off like 47 howitzers." - **San Fernando Valley (CA) Magazine**

"New York's most sought after women find themselves having to make desperate decisions that will affect their very lives." - **Wilmington (DE) News Journal**.

"The novel is rich in esoteric commercial lore about modeling...." **Saturday Review**

"Possibly the most honest novel to appear by a female writer in the past decade."- **Literary Times**

"Crammed with all the ingredients of a blockbuster. ..Beasts in the Beauty Jungle... authentic, searing exposé." **London Evening News**

"Miss Rejaunier is most interesting when she goes behind the scenes in the modeling world." - **Detroit Free Press**

"If a male author had written *The Beauty Trap*, he'd be hanged by the thumbs." - **UPI**

#########

WHAT READERS ARE SAYING ABOUT
THE PLANES OF HEAVEN SERIES

"A new universe of limitless visions and ideas."

"What a priceless gift to share with those who are seeking a spiritual uplift!"

"Ms. Rejaunier has handled this material with rare expertise and dedication. In short, she has accomplished a monumental task."

"What a trip! Author Jeanne Rejaunier takes us on a privileged tour beyond the boundaries of any reality we have previously known."

"One of the most versatile and capable authors living today, Jeanne Rejaunier continues her series about heaven and the hereafter."

"Ms. Rejaunier has handled this material with rare expertise and dedication."

"This book and its previous counterparts are a MARVEL."

"Tour beyond the boundaries of any reality we have previously known. By sharing her privileged experiences with teachers and mystics, the author draws the reader into a new universe of limitless visions and ideas."

"Any reader interested in spirituality, metaphysics, personal development, and self-help would be fascinated by this interesting and compellingly written book."

######

****

The four previous books in the Planes of Heaven series are available internationally, both online and in bookstore chains: *Planes of the Heavenworld; Everything You Always Wanted to Know About Heaven But Didn't Know Where to Ask; The Kingdom of Heaven and 4th Dimensional Consciousness*, and *The Afterlife in the Here and Now.*

#####

Made in the USA
San Bernardino, CA
01 May 2020

70734680R00098